PRACTICAL
FINANCIAL
ANALYSIS

PRACTICAL
FINANCIAL
ANALYSIS

JAMES O GILL

**KOGAN
PAGE**

First published in the United States of America in 1992 entitled *Financial Analysis* by Crisp Publications Inc, 1200 Hamilton Court, Menlo Park, California 94025, USA.

This edition first published in Great Britain in 1993 by Kogan Page Ltd, 120 Pentonville Road, London N1 9JN.

British Library Cataloguing in Publication Data

A CIP record for this book is available from the British Library.

ISBN 0 7494 0890 1

Printed and bound in Great Britain by
Biddles Ltd, Guildford and King's Lynn

◀ CONTENTS ▶

◀ INTRODUCTION ▶

This book is a sequel to *How to Understand Financial Statements*. It is written for someone who has a basic understanding of financial statements, knows the use of ratios, and can analyse expenses. These skills should be reviewed from either reading *How to Understand Financial Statements* or taking a course in basic finance, or both.

Practical Financial Analysis will help the advancing company manager – someone going into middle management who must have a grasp of how decisions affect the income flow. It provides the analytical tools to examine how financial decisions affect ratios such as return on investment and debt to equity. It also presents ways to determine the payback of capital investments and explains how to read an annual report. This book will also benefit any small business that is growing or facing increased competition.

The material and tools presented in this book should be gone over several times. Go through the checklists and work through the sample problems until you understand not only what is happening, but why. Take it step-by-step, and you will achieve a working understanding of each analysis tool. You will also know where and when to apply those tools.

James O Gill

◀ ABOUT THIS BOOK ▶

Business is facing new challenges. International competition, technology that didn't even exist a few years ago, new environmental and safety regulations and global marketing can make it difficult to stay in business, let alone increase your business. You can't stop taking risks, but you can minimise them by giving more attention to the financial implications of each decision.

That's what this book is about. It is designed to provide easy-to-follow instructions to analyse your financial position and make it better. It can also be used as a reference manual. It provides definitions and explains terms that you, as an aspiring manager or small business owner, may hear during meetings or business conversations. It provides examples to increase your understanding, and it will help you to speak with confidence about the affairs of your company.

As you use the tools in this book, you will soon discover which ones are most beneficial to you. Please, do not try to memorise all of them at once. There is no exam at the end of it. These tools are to be applied to the actual situations you encounter in your work. A calculator will be necessary for working through the examples and the review at the end of each chapter.

Goals

The goals of this book are to:

1. Provide a quick review of the basics of financial analysis.
2. Introduce you to the contents of company financial statements.
3. Explain ratios concerning capitalisation.
4. Show various ways that ratios interact when one is changed.
5. Show how to use fast decision-making techniques.
6. Provide tips on how to interpret an annual report.

As a new or experienced manager, the more you understand about the financial side of your business, the better decisions you will make. The more you use the tools contained in this book, the better presentations you will be able to give.

Practical Financial Analysis is designed to teach you how to be a better manager by providing the tools to analyse your part of the business, make better decisions, and help you to understand the terms and language of financial statements and analysis.

◀ CHAPTER 1 ▶

REVIEWING THE BASICS

This chapter is a quick review of the basics covered in my previous book, *How to Understand Financial Statements*. This review will help you to make the transition to understanding more complex balance sheets and profit and loss accounts.

In most company profit and loss accounts, details of expenses are consolidated into just a few figures, so they aren't all presented in an annual report. But an individual manager will usually receive a detailed report on his or her area. If you get them from an internal source and wish to analyse them the analysis techniques are covered in the basic book, *How to Understand Financial Statements* (Kogan Page).

If you are familiar with basic ratio and expense analysis this part of the book will serve as a quick refresher for you, or it may be omitted.

The balance sheet equation

The basic formula is:

Assets = Liabilities including Shareholders' funds (called net worth in the previous book) or, put another way, the equation can be stated as: Net Assets = Shareholders' Funds.

A simple balance sheet is shown on page 12.

The balance sheet shows *assets*, *liabilities*, and *shareholders' funds*.

The value of a shareholder's investment in a company can be equated with the net assets of the company.

XYZ HARDWARE AND BUILDING SUPPLY LIMITED

Balance sheet at the year ended 19XX

	£	£
FIXED ASSETS		
Land and buildings	50,000	
Fixtures and fittings	50,000	
		100,000
CURRENT ASSETS		
Stock	210,000	
Debtors	85,000	
Cash	2,000	
	297,000	
CURRENT LIABILITIES		
Trade creditors	205,000	
Bills payable	18,000	
Accruals	6,000	
	229,000	
NET CURRENT ASSETS		68,000
TOTAL ASSETS		168,000
LONG-TERM LIABILITIES		
Bank loan		25,000
TOTAL NET ASSETS		143,000
SHAREHOLDERS' FUNDS		143,000

The assets are divided into *current assets* and *fixed assets*. The liabilities are divided into *current liabilities* and *long-term liabilities*. The shareholders' funds is the difference between assets and liabilities.

Glossary of balance sheet terms

Accruals

Taxes, wages or utility accounts (eg electricity) that are accumulated against current profits but not yet due to be paid.

Assets
The money, stock, receipts, land, buildings and equipment that a company owns and that have monetary value.

Bills payable
Money borrowed by the company that is to be paid back within one year.

Creditors
Sometimes called trade creditors. These are the total of all monies owed by the company to suppliers or vendors for raw materials, products or merchandise.

Current assets
The sum of cash, notes, and debtors (minus reserves for bad debts), advances on stocks, stocks and any other item that can be converted into cash in the short term, usually defined as less than a year.

Current liabilities
The total of all monies owed by the company that will fall due within one year.

Debtors
The monies owed to the company (but not yet collected) for merchandise, products or services sold or performed.

Depreciation
The estimated decrease in value of a fixed asset over its useful life. This is classified as an expense on the income statement, thus reducing profit. You will learn more about this in Chapter 3.

Fixed assets
Land, buildings, building equipment, fixtures, machinery, tools, furniture and office equipment, cars. These are shown in the balance sheet net of depreciation.

Liabilities

Everything that a company owes to a creditor. Liabilities are the debts owed by the company. They include bills payable, accounts payable, and accruals. There are two categories of liabilities: current liabilities and long-term liabilities.

Long-term liabilities

These represent all the obligations such as mortgages, bonds, fixed-term loans, and any other monies that come due more than one year from the date of the statement.

Mortgage or charge

A legal document that pledges property to cover a debt.

Scrap value

The estimated price for which a fixed asset can be sold at the end of its useful life.

Shareholders' funds

What the owners (the shareholders) have left when all the liabilities have been met. It is represented on a balance sheet as the difference between total assets and total liabilities.

Stock

For a manufacturing firm, it is the sum of finished merchandise on hand, raw material, and work in progress. For retailers and wholesalers, it is the stock of goods on hand that are for sale.

Profit and loss account

The profit and loss account analyses how shareholders' wealth increased or decreased during the year.

Shown opposite is a simple detailed profit and loss account.

Glossary of profit and loss account terms

Cost of sales

For a retail or wholesale business, it is the total price paid for the products sold during the accounting period, plus the cost of having

14

Profit and loss account		
		£
Sales		700,000
Cost of goods sold		500,000
Gross profit		200,000
Expenses	£	
Wages	65,000	
Delivery	7,000	
Bad debt	4,000	
Telephone	2,000	
Depreciation	4,000	
Insurance	7,000	
Rates	8,000	
Interest	8,700	
Advertising	3,000	
Miscellaneous	2,000	
Total Expenses	110,700	
Net Profit		89,300

the products delivered to the store. For a manufacturing firm, it is the opening stock plus purchases, delivery costs, material, labour and overheads, less the closing stock.

Dividend
The portion of a company's net earnings paid to shareholders at a specified rate per share.

Gross profit
The profit before expenses, interest, other charges and corporation tax have been deducted.

Net profit
As used in this book, it refers to the profit after expenses but before paying corporation tax.

JOG Limited – Profit and loss account Year end 19XX	£
Turnover	21,108,000
Cost of sales	13,546,000
Gross profit	7,562,000
Operating expenses	4,958,000
Operating profit	2,604,000
Interest	278,000
Profit before tax	2,326,000
Corporation tax	1,163,000
Profit after taxation	1,163,000
Retained earnings at the beginning of the year	3,080,000
	4,243,000
Dividend (30p per share)	304,000
Retained earnings at the end of the year	£3,939,000

Operating expenses
The cost of doing business. It includes such items as administrative wages, telephone, insurance, depreciation and advertising. Operating expenses are sometimes divided into 'administrative expenses' and 'distribution costs' in the profit and loss account of a company.

Profit after taxation
The amount left over after deducting all due bills for the accounting period and paying off all due interest and corporation tax.

Retained earnings
The portion of a company's net earnings not paid to shareholders in the form of dividends. Retained earnings are reinvested in the company. They accumulate over the life of the company.

Turnover
The value of all sales less returns, allowances, discounts and rebates.

Ratios and percentages

Ratios compare one thing with another. This establishes a relationship or correlation. For instance, if you want to know what percentage of sales the net profit represents, simply divide the sales figure (the base figure) into the amount of net profit. For example, if the sales are £700,000 and the net profit is £15,300, the percentage is:

Ratio analysis allows comparison and interpolation of accounts.

$$\frac{£15,300}{£700,000} \times 100 = 2.2\%$$

The base number need not be the larger number. For example, the ratio of assets to sales: if the sales are £700,000 and the assets are £397,000, the assets generated sales of 1.8 times the assets' value – there is an 'asset turnover' of 1.8 times.

$$\frac{£700,000}{£397,000} = 1.8 \text{ times}$$

Hint: If the top number is smaller than the bottom number, the ratio will be a percentage. If the top number is larger than the bottom number, the ratio will be expressed as 'times'.

Liquidity ratios

Liquidity ratios measure the amount of cash or investments that can be converted to cash in order to pay expenses, bills and other obligations as they come due.

Liquidity ratios can help creditors to decide whether to offer credit terms to the company.

The *current ratio* measures the ability of the company to meet short-term obligations.

$$\text{Current ratio} = \frac{\text{Current assets}}{\text{Current liabilities}}$$

A low current ratio may indicate a lack of capital to pay off debt and to take advantage of discounts.

A high current ratio does not necessarily mean a company is in good shape. It could mean that its cash is not being put to the best use. Also, it does not indicate the state of debtors or stock which may have caused the high ratio.

A quick version of the current ratio eliminates stock (and sometimes accounts receivable) from the current assets. This gives a conservative number. It is sometimes called the quick ratio, or the 'acid test'.

Try both before deciding which version to use, and look closely at debtors and the condition of the stock.

The *turnover of cash ratio* measures the adequacy of the company's working capital, which is required to pay bills and to finance sales. The working capital is the current assets minus the current liabilities.

$$\text{Turnover of cash ratio} \quad = \quad \frac{\text{Sales}}{\text{Working capital}}$$

A low turnover of cash ratio means that you have funds tied up in short-term, low-yielding assets, and you can get by with less cash.

A high ratio could mean an inability to pay your bills.

The *debt to equity (or shareholders' funds) ratio* measures total debt coverage. It expresses the relationship between the capital contributed by the creditors and that contributed by the shareholders.

$$\text{Debt to equity ratio} \quad = \quad \frac{\text{Total debt}}{\text{Equity (shareholders' funds)}}$$

A low debt to equity ratio would indicate that the company could borrow money more easily. It could also mean that the company is too conservative.

A high ratio indicates that most of the risk in the business is assumed by the creditors. Obtaining money from outside sources, such as a bank, will be more difficult.

Liquidity ratios help investors and bankers to decide if the company deserves their money.

Profitability ratios

Profitability ratios measure and help to control income.

Profitability ratios help to determine whether the assets invested in a company are being used efficiently.

The *net profit ratio* measures the effectiveness of management. Filtering out the effects of debt and tax is useful for two reasons. First, tax rates change because of political events rather than due to the success of the business. Second, high debt payments such as those found in new businesses, could distort earnings making comparison with another company not valid.

$$\text{Net profit ratio} = \frac{\text{Profit before interest and taxes (PBIT)}}{\text{Sales}}$$

A low net profit ratio is not good. It could indicate that expenses are too much for the sales volume.

A high ratio indicates either that expenses are being held down or that the company may be getting more out of its assets and debt.

The *rate of return on sales* measures how much net profit was derived from each pound of sales. It can provide an idea of the coverage of fixed costs. It can also indicate whether expenses are being held down.

$$\text{Rate of return on sales} = \frac{\text{Net profit}}{\text{Sales}}$$

A low rate of return on sales is not necessarily bad if your company or industry operates on low margins and high volume.

A high rate is usually good if other things are in line – if payments are kept up, assets are replaced and other expenses are not deferred.

The *return on capital employed* (ROCE) measures how much net profit was derived from the shareholders' investment in the company.

$$\text{Return on capital employed} = \frac{\text{Net profit}}{\text{Shareholders' funds}}$$

A low rate of return on capital employed means that another investment may be better. It could indicate that management is inefficient or that the company is too conservative and not achieving its potential earnings.

A high rate indicates that borrowing may be the source of much of the capitalisation, or that management is extremely efficient, or that the firm is undercapitalised.

The *rate of return on assets* measures the profit that is generated by the assets of the business.

$$\text{Rate of return on assets} \quad = \quad \frac{\text{Net profit}}{\text{Total assets}}$$

A low rate of return on assets indicates poor performance or poor use of the assets by management.

A high rate indicates good performance and good use of assets.

Watch out if the fixed assets of the business are heavily depreciated or there is a large amount of unusual expenses or income.

Efficiency ratios

Obtaining money from debtors is vital to the business.

Efficiency ratios measure how well the business is being conducted. They provide quick indications of how well your credit control policy is working and your stock is moving. They help keep the business in balance.

The following ratio measures the time it takes to collect outstanding debts:

$$\frac{\text{Accounts receivable} \times 365 \text{ days per year}}{\text{Sales}}$$

A high ratio shows that it takes too many days to collect the company's money. This means that cash will be too low and possibly some bills won't get paid.

A low ratio means that debts due from credit sales are being collected promptly and that more money is in the company and working to the shareholders' advantage.

The *stock turnover rate* measures how fast the stock is moving.

$$\text{Stock turnover rate} \quad =$$

$$\frac{\text{Cost of sales}}{\text{Average stockholding} } \quad \text{or} \quad \frac{\text{Sales}}{\text{Average stockholding}}$$

A low rate of stock turnover indicates that too much money may be tied up in goods and storage and not working as hard as it could.

A high rate indicates that sales are booming – or that sales are lost because the merchandise was not available.

The *ratio of fixed assets to net worth (shareholders' funds)* measures the proportion of net worth that is made up of fixed assets. It provides an indication of how much capital is tied up in buildings, fixtures, equipment, etc.

Investors must finance working capital, as well as fixed assets.

$$\text{Fixed assets to net worth ratio} = \frac{\text{Fixed assets}}{\text{Net worth (shareholders' funds)}}$$

A low ratio of fixed assets to net worth indicates that the net worth or shareholders' funds may be more liquid and easier to obtain in the event of bankruptcy or tight financial times.

A high ratio indicates that the shareholders' part of the company may be bricks and mortar or a piece of equipment. The company may be lacking working capital.

The *investment turnover ratio* measures the amount of sales generated by the assets.

$$\text{Investment turnover ratio} = \frac{\text{Sales}}{\text{Total assets}}$$

A low investment turnover ratio may indicate that there are too many assets and too few sales.

A high ratio may mean that something good is happening. The company is experiencing more sales without investing in more equipment or buildings, or obtaining more cash.

21

Review

Do you remember? Write your answers in the spaces provided.

1. The balance sheet equation?

   _____

2. The two types of assets?

   _____

3. The two types of liabilities?

   _____

4. The definition of *debtors*?

   _____

   _____

5. The definition of *stock*?

   _____

   _____

6. The definition of *long-term liabilities*?

   _____

   _____

7. The definition of *cost of sales*?

   _____

   _____

8. The definition of *gross profit*?

   _____

   _____

9. The definition of *net profit*?

   _____

   _____

10. The two ways that ratios are expressed?

    _____

    _____

The answers are on page 24.

Practice problems

Before moving on you may want to brush up on working and interpreting some ratios. Based on the following figures, calculate the ratios indicated below. Give a brief analysis of each ratio you calculate.

Current assets	£524,000	Net profit	£18,000
Current liabilities	£302,000	Total assets	£1,129,000
Sales	£1,545,000	Debtors	£278,000
Working capital (current assets – current liabilities)	£222,000		

Example
Current ratio:

$$\frac{\text{Current assets}}{\text{Current liabilities}} = \frac{£524,000}{£302,000} = 1.7 \text{ times}$$

Analysis: The company is a little short of having a comfortable margin to pay current debts.

1. **Turnover of cash ratio:**
$$\frac{\text{Sales}}{\text{Working capital}} = \underline{\hspace{2cm}} = \underline{\hspace{1cm}} \text{ times}$$
   Analysis: _____

2. **Rate of return on sales:**
$$\frac{\text{Net profit}}{\text{Sales}} = \underline{\hspace{2cm}} = \underline{\hspace{1cm}} \%$$
   Analysis: _____

3. **Rate of return on assets:**
$$\frac{\text{Profit}}{\text{Total assets}} = \underline{\hspace{2cm}} = \underline{\hspace{1cm}} \%$$

Analysis: _____

4. Time to collect outstanding debtors:

$$\frac{\text{Debtors} \times 365}{\text{Sales}} = \underline{\hspace{3cm}} = \quad \text{days}$$

Analysis: _____

5. Investment turnover ratio:

$$\frac{\text{Sales}}{\text{Total assets}} = \underline{\hspace{3cm}} = \quad \text{times}$$

Analysis: _____

The answers are on page 25.

Answers to review

1. Assets = Liabilities + Shareholders' equity (or shareholders' funds)

2. Current assets and fixed assets.

3. Current liabilities and long-term liabilities.

4. *Debtors* are the monies owed to the company (but not yet collected) for merchandise, products, or services sold or performed.

5. *Stock* for a manufacturing firm is the sum of finished merchandise on hand, raw material, and work in progress. For retailers and wholesalers, it is the stock of goods on hand that are for sale.

6. *Long-term liabilities* are all the obligations such as mortgages, bonds, fixed-term loans, and any other monies that come due more than one year from the date of the balance sheet.

7. *Cost of sales*, for a retail or wholesale business, is the total price paid for the products sold during the accounting period plus the cost of having the goods delivered to the store. For a manufacturing firm it is the opening stock plus purchases, delivery costs, material, labour and overheads, less the closing stock.

8. *Gross profit* is the profit before expenses, interest, other charges and corporation tax have been deducted.

9. *Net profit* is the amount left over after paying off all due bills for the accounting period plus interest and other charges, but before paying corporation tax.

10. If the top number is smaller than the bottom number, the ratio will be a percentage. If the top number is larger than the bottom number, the ratio will be expressed as 'times'.

Answers to practice problems

1. $\dfrac{\text{Sales}}{\text{Working capital}} = \dfrac{£1,545,000}{£222,000} = 7.0 \text{ times}$

Analysis: the working capital appears adequate to support the sales volume.

2. $\dfrac{\text{Net profit}}{\text{Sales}} = \dfrac{£18,000}{£1,545,000} = 1.2\%$

Analysis: This is a low profit. Further analysis is warranted to determine why.

3. $\dfrac{\text{Net profit}}{\text{Total assets}} = \dfrac{£18,000}{£1,129,000} = 1.6\%$

Analysis: The company is not getting a good return on its assets.

4. $\dfrac{\text{Debtors} \times 365}{\text{Sales}} = \dfrac{£278,000 \times 365}{£1,545,000} = 66 \text{ days}$

Analysis: The company should tighten up and start collecting these outstanding accounts faster. With more cash, current liabilities may be paid faster and this will improve the current ratio.

5. $\dfrac{\text{Sales}}{\text{Total assets}} = \dfrac{£1,545,000}{£1,129,000} = 1.4 \text{ times}$

Analysis: Too many assets chasing too few sales. The return on assets should be several times higher.

◄ CHAPTER 2 ►

CORPORATE FINANCIAL STATEMENTS

Balance sheet analysis

Being able to dig out information from company accounts is a very valuable skill.

Company balance sheets are not very detailed. It is worth obtaining a copy of your own company's annual report and accounts and using it to practice 'digging out' information.

You will see that most items in the balance sheet have a number next to them which refers to a note at the back of the accounts. All the information you need for balance sheet analysis will be found in the balance sheet or, in more detail, in the notes to the accounts.

By looking at the example of a balance sheet and related notes for JOG Limited below, you will see that information relating to depreciation of fixed assets can be found in note 1. As we work through the example for JOG Limited in this chapter, you would obtain useful practice at 'digging out' information if you worked through your own company's accounts at the same time.

You will notice that the example of a balance sheet which follows contains information for two years: the current year and the previous year. This is necessary to aid interpretation of the company's accounts, particularly whether it is growing or declining.

The balance sheet describes the financial condition of a company as at a particular date. The assets, or those things the company owns and has the right to use, are listed in the top half of the balance sheet. They are usually listed in reverse order of liquidity. Fixed assets, theoretically considered to be illiquid (because the business could not sell them without folding), are at the very top of the balance sheet, land, buildings, plant and machinery, office equipment, company cars and other 'tangibles' are included here. Intangibles such as goodwill are listed next. Stock comes first in the current assets section, then debtors and finally cash.

In the bottom half of the balance sheet are liabilities and shareholders' funds. Those liabilities that must be paid first appear first. Since the shareholders must wait to see if there is any money left before receiving their dividends, the shareholders' funds are shown at the bottom. In the middle is long-term debt.

Begin your analysis by examining the major categories listed above. For instance, JOG Limited's current assets declined slightly from year 1 to year 2. So did fixed assets (property and equipment), and other assets. This in itself appears not too significant. However, cash increased and stocks declined by good-sized margins. This puts the company in a very liquid position. In fact, some more money should go towards any or all of lowering debt, increasing sales, upgrading equipment and facilities or paying higher dividends. Generally this balance sheet shows the company to be too conservative and cash rich.

The balance sheet is a 'snapshot' in time, showing the state of the company at the close of business on a particular day. Things could be very different next day.

JOG Limited

Balance sheet as at 31 December 19X2

	(Note)	19X2 £000	19X2 £000	19X1 £000	19X1 £000
FIXED ASSETS	1		1,154		1,249
CURRENT ASSETS					
Stocks	2	4,565		5,776	
Debtors	3	3,128		3,054	
Short-term investments	4	407		100	
Cash		1,270		773	
		9,370		9,703	

CURRENT LIABILITIES			
Creditors due within one year	5	(1,857)	(2,922)
NET CURRENT LIABILITIES		7,513	6,781
TOTAL ASSETS LESS CURRENT LIABILITIES		8,667	8,030
LONG-TERM LIABILITIES			
Creditors due after more than one year	6	(2,150)	(1,950)
		6,517	6,080
CAPITAL AND RESERVES			
Share capital	7	1,013	1,033
Share premium	8	1,565	1,967
Profit and loss reserve	9	3,939	3,080
		6,517	6,080

Notes to the balance sheet
1. FIXED ASSETS

	Land & buildings	Equipment	Total
	£000	£000	£000
Opening balance	967	1,267	2,234
Disposals	(67)	(110)	(177)
Closing balance	900	1,157	2,057
Depreciation	403	500	903
Net book value	497	657	1,154

2. STOCKS
The figure for stocks can be analysed as follows:

	19X2	19X1
	£000	£000
Raw materials	315	564
Work in progress	775	944
Finished goods	3,475	4,268
	4,565	5,776

3. DEBTORS

The figure for debtors can be analysed as follows:

	19X2	19X1
	£000	£000
Trade debtors	2,958	2,700
Prepayments	114	104
Other debtors	56	250
	3,128	3,054

4. SHORT-TERM INVESTMENTS

	19X2	19X1
	£000	£000
Government securities	407	100

5. CREDITORS (less than one year)

	19X2	19X1
	£000	£000
Bills payable	500	400
Trade creditors	408	873
Corporation tax	500	999
Accruals	449	650
	1,857	2,922

6. CREDITORS (due after more than one year)

	19X2	19X1
	£000	£000
Long-term loans	2,150	1,950

7. SHARE CAPITAL

	19X2 £000	19X1 £000
Ordinary shares at £1 each		
Authorised share capital	2,500	2,500
Fully paid-up	1,033	1,013

8. SHARE PREMIUM ACCOUNT

	£000
Balance at 31 December 19X2	1,967
Repayment of share premium	402
	1,565

9. PROFIT AND LOSS RESERVE

	£000
Retained earnings at 31 December 19X1	3,080
Profit for year	1,163
Dividend	304
Retained earnings at 31 December 19X2	3,939

Analysis

Another way of looking at major categories is to break them down into percentages, like this:

JOG Limited

Current assets	87%	Current liabilities	18%
Fixed assets	11%	Long-term liabilities	20%
Other assets	2%	Shareholders' equity	62%
Total assets	100%	Total liabilities and equity	100%

A safe company has a low return, a large equity base and slow growth, with little debt and short-term assets.

A safe corporation			
Current assets	70%	Current liabilities	25%
Fixed assets	30%	Long-term liabilities	15%
		Shareholders' equity	60%

A risk corporation has a high yield, high long-term assets, outside funds supporting over one-half of the business, a small equity base, fast growth, and large earnings fluctuations.

A risk corporation			
Current assets	30%	Current liabilities	20%
Fixed assets	70%	Long-term liabilities	45%
		Shareholders' equity	35%

Note. Whether these ratios are satisfactory or not will vary considerably depending on the industry.

Is your company safe or is it a risky company? Use the figures from the balance sheet to calculate the percentages.

Risky companies tend to owe more to outsiders than shareholders.

Current assets _____ % Current liabilities _____ %
Fixed assets _____ % Long-term debt _____ %
Other assets _____ % Shareholders' equity _____ %

How would you characterise your company, based on these figures?

_____

_____

_____

_____

Glossary

Ordinary shares
Ownership of ordinary shares usually brings with it voting power in the company. The more shares a shareholder owns the greater his control over the directors and policy of the company.

Par value

The face value of shares at the time they are issued. Subsequent selling prices are usually different from the par value. A stock does not have to have a par value designation.

Preference shares

Usually, dividends are paid to holders of preference shares before they are paid to holders of ordinary shares. Also, if the company declares bankruptcy, holders of preference shares have a claim on the assets of the business before the ordinary shareholders. Preference shares usually carry no voting rights and a fixed level of dividend.

Prepaid expenses

Those expenses that carry into the next accounting period. They may be rents, subscriptions, wages, etc.

Share capital

The total amount invested in the business in exchange for shares of stock up to par value.

Share premium

If, when it's first issued, a stock sells for above its par value, the excess is known as share premium reserve.

Shareholders' funds

The total value of the company's ordinary shares and preference shares, share premium and retained earnings.

These definitions should be checked by your company's accounting people to see if they match the company's usage. If not, use your company's terminology.

Profit and loss account

The profit and loss account reflects the performance of the business over a defined period, usually one year.

The profit and loss account reports on profitability. The first expense is the cost of sales. For most companies cost of sales reflects purchases less returns, discounts and rebates, plus carriage inwards. This figure is added to the opening stock. The next step is to subtract the closing stock. The remainder is cost of sales.

Here is a profit and loss account for JOG Limited.

JOG Limited

Profit and Loss Account

For the year ending 31 December 19XX

		Year 2	Year 1
1.	Turnover	£21,108,000	£15,033,000
2.	Cost of goods sold	13,546,000	9,692,000
3.	Gross profit (1–2)	7,562,000	5,341,000
4.	Operating expenses	4,958,000	3,754,000
5.	Operating profit (3–4)	2,604,000	1,587,000
6.	Interest	278,000	53,000
7.	Profit before tax (5–6)	2,326,000	1,534,000
8.	Corporation tax (50%)	1,163,000	767,000
9.	Profit after tax (7–8)	1,163,000	767,000
10.	Dividend (30p per share)	304,000	309,000
11.	Retained profit for the year (9–10)	859,000	458,000
12.	Retained profit brought forward	3,080,000	2,622,000
	Retained earnings at the end of the year (11 + 12)	£3,939,000	£3,080,000

In year 2, JOG Limited's net earnings were 5.5 per cent of turnover. The cost of sales was 64 per cent of turnover. The gross profit was 36 per cent of turnover. The earnings before tax were 11 per cent of turnover. The company paid dividends of 1.4 per cent of turnover.

Profit and loss reserve

In the profit and loss account you will find a figure for retained profit. An associated note in the back of the accounts will explain the detail of where this figure comes from. It reports on how much of the firm's earnings were kept within the firm instead of being paid out in dividends. It therefore shows the *changes* in the shareholders' funds between balance sheet dates.

Retained profit is an excellent source of investment finance for the future.

Here is the profit and loss reserve for JOG Limited. It presents the information as it would appear in the notes to the accounts.

Profit and loss account note

	£000
Balance as at end of December 19X1	2,622
Retained profit for the year	859
Balance at the end of the year December 19X2	3,080

It would be a useful exercise to place your company's profit and loss reserve figures in here by way of practice at digging out information. Again the figures will be found in a note to the profit retained for the year figure in the profit and loss account.

Your company's profit and loss account note

	£000
Balance at the end of the previous financial year	
Retained profit from the current financial year	
Plus/minus any reserves created	
Plus/minus any revaluations	
Plus/minus any currency movements	
Plus/minus any goodwill	
Balance at the end of the current financial year.	

From the above, and from your own analysis of your company's profit and loss reserve you will notice that the profit and loss reserve contains a number of items with which you will be unfamiliar. It is more important that you understand the basic information being offered in the profit and loss reserve than you tackle every technical accountancy term shown here. A profit and loss reserve is designed to show the overall movement in the shareholders' funds, and that is the main point to consider. Indeed, small businesses will not have many of the items listed in the profit and loss account of a large corporation.

As for the above analysis, do not be deterred by the fact that you may not know the meaning of every term used. Refer to the glossary given here if you wish to know more, but, in the meantime, you should be able to tell easily whether an item shown in your company's profit and loss reserve is good news for your company's shareholders or not.

The statement of retained profit, or the profit and loss account in the notes to the accounts is a very important piece of information for the shareholders. It reflects just how much the company can distribute in the event of a winding up, or just what sort of funds the company has for paying future dividends. If the profit and loss account is adversely affected by revaluations and provisions for items such as goodwill then the company will look like a poor investment since it will have restricted scope for paying dividends in the future.

A healthy profit reserve is a good indicator of the company's future prospects.

Glossary of profit and loss reserve terms

Currency movements

Assets held in foreign currency must be translated into their sterling equivalent at the balance sheet date. If the same asset was worth £2 this year and £2.50 in the previous year it has fallen in value over the year. To show the adverse effect of this on the profit and loss account we subtract the sterling value of the adverse move from the profit reserves. Again, this is because currency valuations result in no real gain or loss of cash. So no distribution can be made in respect of it.

Goodwill

Goodwill is the extra cash a company may pay when it buys another company as an investment. This 'extra' cash is the difference between the net assets of the company purchased and the purchase price. The cost of the investment may be written off over a number of years, say 20, in a similar way to the writing off of depreciation on tangible fixed assets.

Operating expenses

Operating expenses are those incurred by the business in the pursuance of its normal business operations. For example, in a manufacturing business these items of expense will include advertising and marketing costs, electricity charges for lighting, the warehouse insurance in case of fire damage to the stock, etc. They do not include 'finance' costs such as interest on overdrafts or bank loans. Nor do they include extraordinary items such as loss arising from litigation, or anything else unusual. Operating expenses are often divided into administrative expenses and distribution costs.

Operating profit

Operating profit is the profit after charging the operating expenses against the gross profit. Items such as corporation tax do not appear until further down the profit and loss account.

Revaluation reserves

Revaluation reserves are created when a company 'revalues' some of its fixed assets. The impact of this on the profit of the company is favourable if the revaluation is upwards. However, accountancy rules require that it is charged against the profit after the distribution of the dividend has been accounted for. This is because revaluations are only a paper transaction and have no impact on the cash situation of the company. It is therefore considered to be a non-distributable profit. After all, you cannot distribute a dividend in the form of cash you do not have. However, the net assets of the company have increased so the other side of the accounting double entry is shown as a non-distributable addition to the shareholders' wealth.

Cash flow statements

Cash flow statements are a relatively new development. They replace the source and application of funds statement, which has been in use for a very long time. The change to cash flow statements came into effect in March 1992. So if you are using a set of accounts which were prepared before that date you will need to forgo the following analysis.

The basic purpose of the cash flow statement is to reflect the cash position of the company rather than the profits. Profitability can be affected by a number of non-cash items. Depreciation is a relatively arbitrary matter and so profits can be changed without there being a similar effect on cash.

Investors and bankers are ultimately only interested in the cash position of the company. Can it repay the interest it owes the bank, and can it pay the investors a dividend? If the answer is no then the paper profits are not very useful.

In the example cash flow statement below we look at XYZ Limited.

XYZ Limited
Cash flow statement for the year ended 31 December 19X2

	£000	£000
OPERATING ACTIVITIES		
Cash received from customers		10,660
Cash payments to suppliers		3,115
Cash paid to and on behalf of employees		1,122
Other cash payments		(210)
NET CASH FROM OPERATING ACTIVITIES		6,213
RETURNS ON INVESTMENTS AND SERVICING OF FINANCE		
Interest received	880	
Interest paid	(67)	
Dividend paid	(4,431)	
NET CASH OUTFLOW FROM RETURNS ON INVESTMENTS AND SERVICING OF FINANCE		(3,618)
TAXATION		
Corporation tax paid	(1,423)	
ACT paid	(322)	
TAX PAID		(1,745)
INVESTING ACTIVITIES		
Payments to acquire fixed assets	(71)	
Receipts from sale of fixed assets	190	
NET CASH FLOW FROM INVESTING ACTIVITIES		119
NET CASH INFLOW BEFORE FINANCING		969
FINANCING		
Issue of ordinary share capital	1,000	
Expenses paid in connection with share issues	(30)	

NET CASH INFLOW FROM FINANCING	970
INCREASE IN CASH AND CASH EQUIVALENTS	1,939

Notes to the cash flow statement

Every cash flow statement has associated notes which support the figures given on the face of the cash flow. These notes help us to assess where the funds of the business have been deployed. For example, if the cash figure has not matched expectations based on the profit figure we could examine the growth in debtors. If debtors have increased we will have recorded the sales in our profit and loss account, but we will not yet have received the cash. If this is associated with a rush of sales late in the financial year this will be acceptable. But if the sales pattern is such that we would have expected to recoup this cash a long time ago that would give rise to concern.

So we should examine the cash flow statement very carefully together with the associated notes.

The notes to the cash flow will appear something close to the format shown below.

1. Reconciliation of operating profit to the net cash inflow from operating activities

Operating profit	6,766
Depreciation charge	590
Increase in stock	(421)
Increase in debtors	(1,033)
Increase in creditors	311
	6,213

2. Analysis of changes in cash and cash equivalents during the year

Balance at 1 April 1991	776
Net cash inflow	1,939

Balance at 31 December 19X2   2,715

3. Analysis of the balances of cash and cash equivalents as shown in the balance sheet

	19X2	19X2	Movement in year
Cash at bank and in hand	2,251	544	1,707
Short-term investments	464	232	232
	2,715	776	1,939

4. Analysis of change in finance during the year

	Share capital £000
Balance at 31 December 19X1	3,000
Cash inflow from financing	970
Balance at 31 December 19X2	3,970

The above figures give rise to the following question. Why is it that we have an operating profit of £6,766,000 but a net cash increase of only £1,939,000? The following analysis will help to answer the question.

- Debtors have increased greatly compared with last year. This means that although we have made sales we have yet to collect the cash for them. Whether this is a worrying development or not depends on the age of the debts. If they are old debts we need to examine why it is we have failed to collect them. Explanations may include:
  - Our original terms of credit were too generous.
  - Our credit controllers have not been aggressive enough in pursuing slow payers (that is, people who would pay if we threatened them with cutting off their supply or legal action).
  - Some blue-chip companies are notoriously slow payers. It is not that these debts need to be written off, it is just that they are taking advantage of their power over their smaller suppliers.
  - If the customer is not a solvent blue chip we need to decide

whether such a customer is able to pay its debts, and whether we should continue trading with it in the future. In such a case we would also need to examine the impact of any default on our ability to pay our liabilities in the future.

- We have paid a dividend of £4,431,000. If we had not paid the dividend until after the year end our cash balance would be £4,431,000 higher. This accounts for some two-thirds of the difference between the reported profits and the cash balance at the year end. This of course is a very acceptable reason for reducing cash reserves.
- We paid £1,743 in various taxes. The corporation tax element will reflect the tax charge on the previous year's profits.
- Our various expenditures were partially offset by funds received from the issue of share capital. Given that it has occurred during the year this capital expenditure will not have had a full year's impact on the company's revenue as shown in the trading accounts. This would be a point to remember for the following year.

The new cash flow statement has a very useful purpose from the perspective of the financial analyst. It makes life very much easier because it discloses information in a very useful way.

Cash flows generated from operating activities are needed to finance or repay funds obtained from borrowing. The cash flow statement's separation of the operating funds from other funds gives a very good indication of the company's reliance on external funding, for example bank overdrafts or holding company support. This is information that was not available previously and probably reflects the company's gearing more readily than traditional ratios.

Similarly, the split between the operating cash flow and the investment cash flow should, where the company's accounts relate to one project, give a good indication of the return from an investment, in cash terms.

When dealing with smaller companies it is worth turning to the notes to the cash flow statement to examine the details of cash received from customers, and paid to creditors and employees. This would allow a very quick analysis of the liquidity of the smaller company. Simply put, are they collecting their cash fast enough to cover their regular outgoings?

But not all companies are the same. Some companies can have an apparently very healthy cash situation but in fact be in a bad state of decline. If there is a lot of cash for the apparent profit that the company has reported it usually means that the company has a high proportion of fixed assets to current assets. The discrepancy will result from the fact that a company with a lot of fixed assets will need to charge a lot of depreciation against the profit and loss account.

If there are not the sales to match the depreciation write-off the project, or the company, will be in danger of failing. Yet its cash position looks apparently quite healthy. The reverse is also true. A company with a low level of fixed assets may have an apparently unhealthy cash position but be much more favourably placed to expand.

Checklist

Did you . . .

- Remember that a balance sheet describes the financial condition of a company as of a particular date?
- Remember to begin your analysis by examining the major categories?
- Remember the definition of a safe company?
- Understand the relationship between net assets and shareholders' funds?
- Note that the profit and loss account and statement of retained profits contain the retained profits and dividends paid?
- Remember that the statement of retained earnings reports how much of the company's earnings were not paid out in dividends?
- Remember that there is a difference between the profit reported on the income statement and the cash shown on the balance sheet?
- Use the source and application of funds statement to help determine what the company did and what it did it with?
- Remember that the statement of source and application of funds reports the impact of a company's operating, investing and financing activities on the cash position of a company over an accounting period?

◄ CHAPTER 3 ►

ASSET MANAGEMENT

Management of current assets

Look closely at the current assets of a company. Ask yourself 'can it pay its debts next month'?

The current assets presented here are debtors and stock.

Current assets are important to the company. They pay the bills that flow in from purchases of raw materials, wages, rent, etc. Without sufficient current assets the company could not survive. The cash account and the marketable securities account contain all the 'real' money the corporation has. True, debtors presumably will be paid – but as of the date of the balance sheet, they have not been. Stocks may or may not be sold for the amount shown on the balance sheet; only time will tell. For service businesses, stock is probably not a factor.

Debtor management policies

Let's look at what might happen if JOG Limited tries to increase sales by easing its credit policy. All sales made by JOG Limited are credit sales. The company has no cash sales.

Every sale must be matched by cash, otherwise it is worthless.

If sales rise, so will expenses. Labour, material, cost of financing or carrying the extra credit, and probably bad debts will increase. The question is, will it be worth the expense to ease the restrictions on granting credit as a means to gain higher sales? Nothing else will be changed – advertising will be the same, so will the sales force and the equipment.

The things that must be considered are:

- Projected additional sales
- Discounts for early payment: 2 per cent if paid within 10 days
- Increase in late payments (what percentage of sales and for what length of time)
- Increase in stocks (and all associated costs)
- How to finance (equity or debt)
- Whether there is excess manufacturing capacity (and trained operators)
- Opportunity costs (the loss of other projects which may be able to use the new capital required for this project)
- Increase in bad debts (what percentage of sales).

In the example below, operating expenses are held at a constant percentage of sales (which may not always happen). Even so, the increase in bad debt, the carrying of debtors, the credit operations and allowing a discount to encourage faster payment caused a drop in income as a percentage of sales of 1.2 per cent. This equates to £372,000.

	JOG Limited				
	Projected analysis of credit policy on Debtors Profit				
	End of Year 3				
	Projected income: Old policy *(000)*	**Percentage of sales**	**Effect of policy change** *(000)*	**Projected income: New policy** *(000)*	**Percentage of sales**
Sales	£25,000	100.0	£6,000	£31,000	100.0
Cost of goods sold	16,000	64.0	3,840	19,840	64.0
Gross profit before discounts	9,000	36.0	2,160	11,160	36.0

Minus discounts	0	0	372	372	1.2
Gross profits	9,000	36.0	1,778	10,778	34.8
Operating expenses	5,250	21.0	1,260	6,510	21.0
Profit before credit costs and tax	3,750	15.0	528	4,278	13.8
Credit operation expenses	250	1.0	175	93	0.3
Cost of carrying debtors	202	0.8	119	321	1.1
Bad debt losses	100	0.4	520	620	2.0
Profit before taxes	3,198	12.8	46	3,244	10.4
Tax (at 50%)	1,599	6.4	23	1,622	5.2
Net income	1,599	6.4	23	1,622	5.2

JOG Limited notes
(see statement on page 43)
Discounts are 2 per cent if paid within 10 days. It is estimated that 60 per cent of the customers will take them.

$$£31,000,000 × 0.60 × 0.02 = £372,000$$

It is also estimated that 20 per cent of the customers will pay on time (30–40 days), 18 per cent will pay late (over 40 days), and 2 per cent will not pay (up from 0.4 per cent).

The cost of credit operations will be reduced, because of less emphasis on checking references and lax debt collection.

Last year's average collection period for debtors was 51 days. If nothing else changes, the expected average will be 49 days. Under the new policy the average will jump to 63 days. In general, the lower the average collection period, the better.

Another important indicator is the turnover of debtors. It measures how fast your debtors are being collected. Usually, the higher the ratio, the better. The way to determine this ratio is to divide the annual sales by the average debtors.

Under the old policy:

$$\frac{£25,000,000}{£3,354,000} = 7.5 \text{ times}$$

Under the new policy:

$$\frac{£31,000,000}{£5,354,000} = 5.7 \text{ times}$$

JOG Limited currently has a turnover of 7.1 times, or 51 days to collect. The expected increase to 7.5 times (49 days) is better than last year. But under the new policy it falls to 5.7 times, or 63 days. This is a trend in the wrong direction. Even though the company has a high liquidity position, this may not be the best way for it to invest the shareholders' money. Perhaps JOG Limited would be better off to concentrate on spending a little more time and money collecting its current debtors instead of trying to increase sales by increasing debtors. Remember, it's the cash that's collected, not the sales made, that counts.

The average debtors figure is calculated by adding the debtors figure at the beginning of the year to that at the end of the year and dividing by 2.

$$\frac{\text{Debtors at the beginning of the year} + \text{Debtors at the end of year}}{2} = \text{Average debtors}$$

$$\frac{£2,958,000 + £3,750,000}{2} = £3,354,000$$

$$\frac{£2,958,000 + £7,750,000}{2} = £5,354,000$$

Variable costs are 60 per cent and the cost of funds to the corporation is

10 per cent. Only variable expenses are considered because there will be no purchase of equipment to support the increase in sales.

The cost of carrying debtors is determined by:

Average debtors × Variable cost ratio × Cost of funds

£3,354 × 0.60 × 0.10 = £202,000

£5,354 × 0.60 × 0.10 = £321,000

The projected analysis allows us to assess the effects of our policy without trial and error. However, these projected statements are based on assumptions that may turn out to be incorrect. A manager must use experience and judgement along with these indicators.

The figure for average debtors can be misleading if taken from an annual report, where management normally strives to make a good showing. Depending on the industry, debtors will vary during the business cycle. A business will usually end its fiscal year at the end of its business cycle – when the corporation is in a high cash position and has low debtors (and low stock, which is discussed in the next section).

Projected analysis for your company
Try this analysis using your company's data.

Write the figures for your company in the spaces below:
Projected sales £ _____

Discounts £ _____

Increase in late payments _____ %

Increase in stocks £ _____

How to finance: Debt? _____ Equity? _____

Is there excess manufacturing or other required capacity?
          Yes _____ No _____

Any lost opportunity costs? Yes_____ No_____

Have they been evaluated? Yes_____ No _____

Results _____
_____
_____
_____

Will there be an increase in bad debts? Yes_____ No _____

If yes, by how much? £ _____

	Projected income: Old policy (000)	Percent-age of sales	Effect of policy change (000)	Projected income: New policy (000)	Percent-age of sales
Projected analysis of credit policy on debtors End of Year _____					
Sales	_____	_____	100%	_____	_____
Cost of sales	══════	_____	══════	══════	_____
Gross profit before dis-counts	_____	_____	_____	_____	_____
Minus dis-counts	_____	_____	_____	══════	_____
Gross profits	_____	_____	_____	_____	_____
Operating expenses	══════	_____	_____	══════	_____
Profit before credit costs and taxes	══════	_____	══════	══════	_____
Credit oper-ation expenses	_____	_____	_____	_____	_____
Cost of carry-ing debtors	_____	_____	_____	_____	_____
Bad debt losses	══════	_____	══════	══════	_____
Profit before tax	_____	_____	_____	_____	_____
Tax	_____	_____	_____	_____	_____
Net income	_____	_____	_____	_____	_____

What percentage increase? _____ %

Will credit operation expenses rise or fall? _____

By how much? £_____, or_____%

Will cost of carrying debtors rise?   Yes _____   No _____

By how much? £_____, or_____%

Calculations

Average debtors = Debtors at the beginning of the accounting period + Debtors at the end of the accounting period ÷ 2.

Current policy:

$$£\underline{\hspace{3cm}+£\hspace{3cm}} = £\underline{\hspace{5cm}}$$
$$2$$

New policy:

$$£\underline{\hspace{3cm}+£\hspace{3cm}} = £\underline{\hspace{5cm}}$$
$$2$$

$$\text{Debtor turnover} = \frac{\text{Annual sales}}{\text{Average debtors}}$$

Current policy:

$$\frac{£\underline{\hspace{2cm}}}{£} = £\underline{\hspace{3cm}}$$

New Policy:

$$\frac{£\underline{\hspace{2cm}}}{£} = £\underline{\hspace{3cm}}$$

Cost of carrying debtors = Average debtors × Variable cost ratio × Cost of funds. The variable cost ratio is determined from your company's expenses. The cost of funds is determined by your company.

Current policy:

$$£\underline{\hspace{3cm}} \times \underline{\hspace{2cm}}\% \times \underline{\hspace{1.5cm}}\% = £\underline{\hspace{2cm}}$$

New policy:

$$£\underline{\hspace{3cm}} \times \underline{\hspace{2cm}}\% \times \underline{\hspace{1.5cm}}\% = £\underline{\hspace{2cm}}$$

Stock valuation methods

In this section we will look at ways of valuing stock through the accounting techniques of the average cost method, FIFO (first in-first out), and LIFO (last in-first out).

Stock valuation can greatly change the final profit figure.

1. The average cost method

Divide the total number of goods available for sale into the average purchase cost for the period of time under examination. This cost should include inward freight and delivery charges to get the raw material to the manufacturer or the goods from the supplier. The total number of goods that have been sold during this period divided by the same average cost would equate to the cost of sales.

Example
Three items are in stock. If the first item cost £100, the second cost £300, and the third cost £500, what is the average cost of sales? If two of these units are sold, what is the average remaining stock valuation?
The average purchase cost would be:

$$\frac{£100 + £300 + £500}{3} = \frac{£900}{3} = £300$$

So the cost of goods sold is £300 × 2 = £600. The remaining stock valuation is £300 per unit.

2. FIFO

The FIFO (first in-first out) method is based on the assumption that the stock acquired first is the first used or sold. Therefore, the remaining stock consists of the most recently purchased items. This method will reflect the most recent cost of the stock on a balance sheet. The cost of sales will reflect the earliest cost of purchases.

Example
Three items are in stock. The first to be purchased cost £100, the second £300, and the third £500. What is the cost of sales sold? If two of these items are sold, what is the value of the remaining stock?

The cost of sales is £100 + £300 = £400. The value of the remaining stock is £500 per unit.

3. LIFO

The LIFO (last in-first out) method is based on the assumption that the stock acquired last is the first used or sold. Therefore, the remaining stock consists of the oldest or first purchased items. This method will reflect the earliest cost of the stock on the balance sheet. The cost of sales will reflect the most recent prices.

Example
The same three items are in stock. The cost of the first item to be purchased was £100, the cost of the second £300, and the cost of the third £500. What is the cost of sales? If two of these items are sold, what is the value of the remaining stock?

The cost of goods sold is £500 + £300 = £800. The remaining inventory is valued at £100.

The purpose of using these stock valuation methods can be to reduce tax liability. From the following example, we see that during a period of rising prices (reflected in the cost of goods sold), LIFO would reduce the company's corporation tax liability and FIFO would increase it.

	Average cost method	FIFO	LIFO
Opening stock	£10,000	£10,000	£10,000
Purchases	12,000	12,000	12,000
Goods for sale	22,000	22,000	22,000
Sales	15,000	15,000	15,000
Cost of sales	11,000	10,000	12,000
Closing stock (cost of goods sold minus goods for sale)	11,000	12,000	10,000
Profit (cost of goods sold minus sales)	4,000	5,000	3,000
Taxation (at 50%)	2,000	2,500	1,500
Profit after tax	2,000	2,500	1,500

In this example, it is assumed that the average cost method provides the best measure of performance. So the tax is subtracted from £4,000 (the profit as calculated by the average cost method). Therefore the lowest figure for taxation – that shown by LIFO – gives the best real earnings in this example.

In a period of declining prices, FIFO would reduce the corporation tax payment and LIFO would increase it.

The method most likely to reflect the real value of stock will depend upon the nature of the goods your company trades in. For example LIFO would be unsuitable for perishable foods. Movements in the market price of stock items will also determine which method of valuation is most suitable. FIFO would be suitable for items which have seen large price movements over the accounting period.

Valuing your company's stock
Fill in the figures for your company.

	Average cost method	FIFO	LIFO
Opening stock			
Purchases			
Goods for sale			
Sales			
Cost of sales			
Closing stock (cost of goods sold minus goods for sale)			
Profit (cost of goods sold minus sales)			
Tax			
Profit after tax			

Which method gives best real profit for your company?

Depreciation

This section covers one aspect of fixed asset valuation called depreciation. Depreciation is a non-cash expense which allocates the cost of assets to succeeding periods of production. Also since both production plants and equipment wear out or become technologically obsolete, depreciation provides a means of devaluing fixed assets.

Depreciation is a method of writing off the cost of purchasing a fixed asset over its useful life.

51

A reduction of the value of a fixed asset through depreciation results in a reduction of shareholders' equity on the balance sheet. Depreciation appears in the profit and loss account either in the cost of sales or as an administrative expense.

There are two main ways of calculating depreciation: the straight-line method and the reducing balance method.

Straight-line method
The simplest and most common way is the straight-line method. To use it, divide the estimated useful life of an asset into its purchase price minus any scrap or resale value.

Example
A piece of equipment has a useful life of five years. It cost £6,000 and it has a resale value of £1,000. What is the yearly depreciation?

Subtract the £1,000 resale price from the cost (£6,000). Divide the remaining £5,000 by 5 years. The depreciation is £1,000 per year for the next five years. This amounts to 16.6 per cent per year. In three years the accumulated depreciation would be £3,000.

The reducing balance method
This method is slightly more complicated. It assumes that the value of an asset declines at the same percentage rate of 'net book value' each year and not at the same absolute figure each year. Net book value is the actual cost of the asset less its depreciation accumulated to date against the asset.

When comparing the asset values or profits of one company with another it will be useful to check depreciation has been charged on the same basis in both companies.

The following is a typical example of how to calculate the depreciation charge for the year on a particular asset using the reducing balance method. Let us say that our company purchases an asset for £6,000. We have decided that the depreciation rate should be 20 per cent. In the first year of business the depreciation charge will be:

$$£6,000 \times 20\% = £1,200$$

In the second year the depreciation charge is calculated by taking the net book value at the end of the previous year and deducting a further 20 per cent from it.

£6,000 − £1,200 = £4,800
£4,800 × 20% = £960

The net book value at the end of year 2 is £4,800 − £960 = £3,840. In the third year of the asset's life we produce a similar calculation again, the net book value of the asset less the depreciation rate of 20 per cent.

£3,840 × 20% = £768

This leaves a net book value of £3,072.

And so it goes on for the remaining life of the asset.

As you will see, the reducing balance method is a 'slower' method of calculating the depreciation charge in so far as it reduces the value of the asset in the books over a longer period.

These two methods (the reducing balance method and the straight-line method) are the only depreciation methods allowed under UK accountancy regulations as set by the accountancy profession. Other countries may do things slightly differently, but their methods are not relevant to the UK.

Review

For each statement below, indicate whether A or B is correct. Tick the appropriate box.

1. Current assets are important because
   □   A. they pay the bills.
   □   B. they look good on a balance sheet.

2. An important item to consider when changing credit policy is
   □   A. the amount spent on advertising.
   □   B. projected additional sales.

3. The method to determine the turnover of debtors is
   □   A. divide total credit sales by average debtors.
   □   B. multiply credit sales by debtors.

4. Debtors are
- ☐ A. better than cash.
- ☐ B. one part of current assets.

5. In determining the effect of a new credit policy to increase sales, only variable expenses are considered because
- ☐ A. they are the only kind a company has.
- ☐ B. fixed expenses are usually not affected by an increase in sales.

Answers: 1 A, 2 B, 3 A, 4 B, 5 B.

For each statement below, circle T if you think it's true, or F if you think it's false.

True or False?

1. If we do the accounts correctly we don't have to worry about having good judgement.   T   F

2. The balance sheet, profit and loss account, and analysis of credit projections are always totally accurate for every company.   T   F

3. FIFO is a type of tax.   T   F

4. The average cost method usually provides the best measure of performance.   T   F

5. During rising prices, LIFO would reduce reported income.   T   F

6. Depreciation is a non-cash expense.   T   F

7. The straight-line method of depreciation is complex and seldom used.   T   F

8. The reducing balance method allows depreciation to be written off against an asset over a longer period of time than the straight-line method would allow.   T   F

Answers: 1 F, 2 F, 3 F, 4 F, 5 F, 6 F, 7 F, 8 T.

◀ CHAPTER 4 ▶

RATIOS

Ratios help to make decisions

Company financial statements (unlike those for partnerships and sole proprietors) include share capital. The management of the company must report to its owners, the shareholders, how the company is doing. One of the techniques used is share capital ratios. Management must also exercise care in the handling of debt and the use of ratios helps them do this.

This part of the book introduces ratios that will help a manager to make decisions regarding the use of debt and equity. There are four equity ratios and one additional debt ratio that help to gauge whether interest payments are covered by the profits of the company.

The total of company debts needs to be balanced by sufficient fixed assets. If not, things are getting risky.

Share capital ratios

In the process of starting a business, all the money from the sale of shares would be shown as 'Share capital' as paid-up capital or ordinary shares, and under 'Current assets' as cash. If the company is ongoing, there will probably be some amount in 'Retained profits'.

The value of a share in the company is the amount a buyer is willing to pay for it. For companies listed on a stock exchange, this is the market value. Several factors make up this price. Those looking for

Share capital ratios help to determine the value of the company to the investor.

income would be interested in the dividends paid; those looking for future growth would be interested in future earnings.

Share capital ratios are (1) return on equity, which indicates the return on the shareholder's investment, (2) the price-earnings ratio, which is used to determine the amount potential investors are willing to pay before investing, (3) the capitalisation rate, which is the reciprocal of the price-earnings ratio; it measures the rate of return the market demands, and (4) the earnings per share ratio measures the earnings for each ordinary share; this is the amount available to each shareholder if management chooses to pay it all out.

We now return to JOG Limited's balance sheet and profit and loss account. The ratios will be calculated using the figures from these accounts.

JOG Limited
Balance sheet as at 31 December 19X2

	£000	£000
Fixed Assets		1,154
Current Assets		
Stocks	4,565	
Debtors	3,128	
Short-term investments	407	
Cash	1,270	
	9,370	
Current Liabilities		
Creditors due within one year	1,857	
Net Current Assets		7,513
Total Assets Less Current Liabilities		8,667
Long-Term Liabilities		
Creditors due after more than one year		2,150
		6,517
Capital and Reserves		
Share capital		1,013
Share premium		1,565

Profit and loss reserve	3,939
	6,517

JOG Limited

Profit and loss account for the Year ended 31 December 19X2

	£000
Turnover	21,108
Cost of sales	(13,546)
Gross profit	7,562
Operating expenses	(4,958)
Operating profit	2,604
Interest	(278)
Profit before taxation	2,326
Taxation (@50%)	1,163
Profit after taxation	1,163
Dividend	304
Retained profit for the year	859
Retained profit brought forward	3,080
Retained profit carried forward	3,939

Return on capital employed

The *return on capital employed* (ROCE) measures the return on the shareholders' investment. It indicates how well management is utilising the owners' investment.

$$\text{Return on equity} = \frac{\text{Profit after tax}}{\text{Shareholders' funds}} \quad \frac{£1,163,000}{£6,517,000} = 17.8\%$$

Would the investors' money be better in a building society or bank? Do the ROCE ratio and if it turns out less than the current rate of interest the answer is 'yes'.

A low ratio means the owners or investors can make more money by investing in something else. However, this ratio should be considered in the light of what has happened during the business cycle, such as expansion, taking on debt or changes in the economy.

A high ratio means management has done well (or they are hiding something until after the annual report). In general, the higher the better.

This ratio is related to the *return on assets* (ROA) when it is modified by an operating ratio and the equity multiplier. It will change due to variance in the turnover of operating assets, operating profit, and the equity multiplier.* (PBIT is *profit before interest and tax,* also called operating profit in the profit and loss account. Net earnings are profits after tax and interest.)

Return on assets × Operating ratio × Equity multiplier

$$= \frac{\text{PBIT}}{\text{Total assets}} \times \frac{\text{Net earnings}}{\text{PBIT}} \times \frac{\text{Total assets}}{\text{Shareholders' funds}}$$

$$= \frac{£2,604,000}{£10,524,000} \times \frac{£1,163,000}{£2,604,000} \times \frac{£10,524,000}{£6,517,000}$$

$$= 0.25 \times 0.45 \times 1.6 = 18\%$$

Earnings per share ratio

The *earnings per share ratio* measures management's success in achieving profits for the owners. This is the amount available to the ordinary shareholder after the payment of all charges and tax for the accounting period.

Earnings per share is very important if the company intends to issue new shares.

$$\text{Earnings per share ratio} = \frac{\text{Profit after tax}}{\text{Number of ordinary shares}} =$$

$$\frac{£1,163,000}{£1,013,000} = £1.15$$

A low ratio means the management is not performing well with regard to earnings.

A high ratio means the shares have a high rate of return. Such shares will generally trade at a higher multiple of its book value than shares with a low rate of return.

The usefulness of this ratio is questionable. There is little or no relationship between book value (based on historical costs) and market value (based on future earning and dividends). However, some analysts use this ratio in connection with one called the market to book value ratio. It looks like this:

---

* It is called an equity multiplier because debt is also used to finance the assets, but it all belongs to the shareholders.

$$\frac{\text{Market price per share}}{\text{Book value per share}}$$

This ratio tells if the market price is higher than book value and by how many times, or if it is lower and by what percentage.

Price/earnings ratio

The *price/earnings ratio* (P/E) measures how much the investors are willing to pay for shares in the company per pound of reported profits.

Safe, blue-chip companies will have higher P/E ratios than small risky companies.

$$\text{Price/earnings ratio} = \frac{\text{Market price per share}}{\text{Earnings per share}} =$$

$$\frac{£10.00}{£1.15} = 8.7 \text{ times}$$

At the current earnings rate an investor 'gets' his money in 8.7 years, either in dividends or in increased book value, if not market value.

A low ratio means the investors are not willing to pay very much for a share. The potential shareholders consider the company to be risky. However, if an investor wants these shares and believes they will grow, the lower the ratio the better for that investor. A low ratio could also mean that a good market has not been developed for this share.

A high ratio means the investors believe that the company has a high growth potential, other things being equal. But if the ratio is too high, investors may look for something more reasonable.

This ratio and the others in this section provide an indication to management of what the investors think about the company – its current, past and future performance. Generally, if all the ratios are showing good, steady performance, the stock will be high.

Capitalisation rate

The capitalisation rate, or rate of return ratio, measures the rate of return that the market demands for the company. As the price/earnings ratio increases, the capitalisation rate decreases.

$$\text{Capitalisation rate} = \frac{\text{Earnings per share}}{\text{Market price per share}} =$$

$$\frac{£1.15}{£10.00} = 11.5\%$$

A low ratio means the investors don't demand a very high return on their money because they consider the company to be a safe investment.

A high ratio means the investors want a high return for each pound invested. In other words it takes a large payoff to attract investors.

Companies which have high earnings growth generally have high prices in relation to earnings, and vice versa. The capitalisation rate reports this in terms of a percentage return based on the selling price of a share and the amount that the company earned on that share.

Debt coverage ratios

Can the company pay the interest on its debts? What if rates are rising?

Debt coverage ratios provide indications of a company's vulnerability to risk. The debt to net assets ratio (presented in Chapter 1) and the ratio shown below provide the necessary tools to evaluate the company's safety.

The *interest cover ratio* measures the extent that operating income can decline before the firm is unable to meet its annual interest charges.

$$\text{Interest cover ratio} = \frac{\text{Profit before interest and taxes}}{\text{Interest}} = \frac{£2,604,000}{£278,000} = 9.4 \text{ times}$$

The generally accepted standard depends on the industry, but a minimum of 2 times is generally required by banks.

A low ratio means a low margin of safety. The company may have difficulty borrowing.

A high ratio means the company probably has spare borrowing capacity.

A variation of this ratio is to add non-cash charges such as depreciation, amortisation and depletion to net profit for cash flow coverage.

$$\frac{\text{Net profit} + \text{Depreciation}}{\text{Interest}} = \frac{£1,163,000 + £903,000}{£278,000} = 7.7 \text{ times}$$

Other fixed charges that must be paid to stay in business, such as rent, should be added to the interest payments.

Another variation is called the fixed charge coverage. This ratio recognises that many companies lease assets and sometimes incur long-term obligations through the lease agreements. If your company uses or is beginning to use leasing, this ratio may make more sense than the interest cover ratio.

It looks like this:

$$\text{Fixed charge coverage} = \frac{\text{PBIT} + \text{lease payments}}{\text{Interest charges} + \text{lease payments}}$$

Limitations of ratio analysis

Ratios are more useful for small, focused companies and fairly autonomous divisions of large corporations. Ratios don't tell too much about a consolidated statement of a large international corporation.

Ratios are no substitute for insight, judgement and objective thinking. A company may change over time, making past ratios of doubtful value. Also, comparing companies of different ages is not very meaningful. Likewise, seasonal factors, unexpected disasters or windfall profits can greatly distort ratios and make comparisons difficult.

Other things which can distort ratios are different means of accounting for expenses, the fact that a company may be making a lot of money from investments rather than its own operation, and a particular company's strategic plans – they may want to have a low profitability now as they are building for the future. And leasing, renting, borrowing and payment practices can make ratios look good for this accounting period but not the next.

Ratios should always be compared to those of other firms in the same industry. This can be done fairly easily, as several companies publish comparative ratio analyses.

Do the ratio analysis, and then apply some common sense and general economic knowledge.

Remember that ratios are ball-park estimates. Ratios cannot consistently provide complete, detailed and accurate data. If they could, we wouldn't need good management.

The main benefit of ratios is to track trends from one accounting period to the next.

Review

For each statement below, write **T** for true or **F** for false.

1. The return on capital employed ratio measures the return on the shareholders' investment.

2. The company's management wants earnings per share to be high.

3. The price/earnings ratio measures how much investors are willing to pay per pound of reported profits.

4. The price/earnings ratio is sometimes called the capitalisation ratio.

5. A high interest cover ratio is not good for the creditors of the company.

6. Ratios are more useful for small, focused companies than large, diverse corporations.

7. By using ratios you don't need good business judgement.

8. Better comparisons of corporate ratios are made if the corporations are in the same industry.

Answers: 1 T, 2 T, 3 T, 4 F, 5 F, 6 T, 7 F, 8 T.

◄ CHAPTER 5 ►

THE INTERACTION OF RATIOS

If one ratio is changed the chances are another will be affected. So it is important to look at all affected ratios. By doing this you can see, on paper, what would happen to your total business if a particular ratio changed. Then you can decide whether you want to take steps to make the new ratio happen.

Perform ratio analysis on all affected ratios.

Changes will also occur during the course of doing business. These changes may be good or not so good. Ratios help to track and determine what is causing these changes.

This chapter describes some of the ways to evaluate changes through ratio analysis, and to understand what might happen to other ratios if we cause one to look good. The ratios are the liquidity, profitability and efficiency ratios from Chapter 1 and the times interest earned ratio from Chapter 4.

The ratios are:

$$\frac{\text{Current assets}}{\text{Current liabilities}}$$

$$\frac{\text{Net profit}}{\text{Total assets}}$$

$$\frac{\text{Total debt}}{\text{Shareholders' funds}}$$

$$\frac{\text{Net profit (PBIT)}}{\text{Sales}}$$

$$\frac{\text{PBIT}}{\text{Interest}} \qquad\qquad \frac{\text{Sales}}{\text{Average stock}}$$

$$\frac{\text{Debtors} \times 365}{\text{Sales}} \qquad\qquad \frac{\text{Sales}}{\text{Total assets}}$$

$$\frac{\text{Profit}}{\text{Shareholders' equity}} \qquad\qquad \frac{\text{Fixed assets}}{\text{Shareholders' equity}}$$

$$\frac{\text{Sales}}{\text{Working capital}}$$

Notes

PBIT = Profit Before Interest and Tax.
Net Profit and PBIT over Sales will be considered as one ratio rather than two for this exercise.

There are five* ratios that have sales as either the numerator or denominator, three ratios that have net profit as the numerator, and three that have shareholders' funds as the denominator.

If one part of a ratio is changed and that part appears in another ratio, that other ratio will change also. For example, one of the most used indicators is the return on capital employed ratio. Suppose the net profit or PBIT (profit before interest and tax) is £2,000, and the shareholders' equity is £10,000.

$$\text{Return on capital employed ratio} \ = \ \frac{\text{Net profit or PBIT}}{\text{Shareholders' funds}} \ =$$

$$\frac{£2,000}{£10,000} = 20\%$$

If you want to increase this ratio to 30 per cent, you can either increase profits by increasing prices or sales, lowering expenses, or lower the shareholders' funds by increasing liabilities or reducing assets. Either

Accountancy involves 'double' entry. A change in one balance will affect another. It's no use improving one ratio if it worsens the overall picture.

---

* Two ratios are treated as one for this exercise: the net profit over sales ratio and the PBIT over sales ratio.

$$\frac{£3,000}{£10,000} = 30\%$$

or

$$\frac{£2,000}{£6,600} = 30\%$$

What happens to the other ratios when prices are raised or expenses lowered? Two other ratios are affected:

Rate of return on sales $\quad = \dfrac{\text{Net profit}}{\text{Sales}} \quad = \quad$ higher

Rate of return on assets $\quad = \dfrac{\text{Net profit}}{\text{Total assets}} \quad = \quad$ higher

Generally, if these ratios are higher the company would receive a better return on sales and a better return on assets.

What if shareholders' funds drops? Two other ratios are affected.

Debt to net worth ratio $= \dfrac{\text{Total debt}}{\text{Shareholders' funds}} =$ higher

Fixed assets to net worth ratio $= \dfrac{\text{Fixed assets}}{\text{Shareholders' funds}} =$ higher

In this case, higher is not better. It shows that debt increased as a percentage of shareholders' funds and that fixed assets increased as a part of shareholders' funds. This means that the shareholders' funds is less liquid and more is tied up in fixed assets.

These are the exercises to go through when trying to change the ratio. A change in one ratio may not be good for the business, or it may call for a less drastic change to be made in order to maintain a balance.

Another example is a change in net sales. Suppose the net profit is £2,000 and the sales are £20,000.

Rate of return on sales $\quad = \dfrac{\text{Net profit}}{\text{Sales}} = \dfrac{£2,000}{£20,000} = \quad 10\%$

Say that you want to raise this ratio to 20 per cent. You could either double the profit from the same sales, or you could cut the sales in

PBIT is the ratio that financial analysts will look at first.

half! (In reality, it's highly unlikely that you could support the same profit on half the sales. But we'll go through this as an exercise.)

If the net profit is doubled or the sales halved, two ratios will be affected.

PBIT is the same as net profit before interest and tax and it responds like the original ratio:

$$\frac{\text{PBIT}}{\text{Sales}} = \text{higher}$$

Debtors turnover is higher, which is not good.

$$\frac{\text{Debtors} \times 365}{\text{Sales}} = \text{higher}$$

If the sales are reduced, three other ratios will be affected.

The investment turnover ratio is lower, which is not good.

$$\frac{\text{Sales}}{\text{Total assets}} = \text{lower}$$

The turnover of cash ratio is lower, which means you don't need so much liquidity to support the amount of sales. In other words, you have cash that isn't properly working for you.

$$\frac{\text{Sales}}{\text{Working capital}} = \text{lower}$$

The stock turnover ratio is also lower, which indicates too much stock to support the lower sales amount.

$$\frac{\text{Sales}}{\text{Average stock}} = \text{lower}$$

Below is a diagram of how the ratios are related. This network of interrelationships illustrates which ratios are affected directly and indirectly when either the numerator or denominator is changed. The ratios connected by a solid line are the ones directly affected. The ratios connected by a dashed line are the ones indirectly affected.

Network of ratio interrelationships

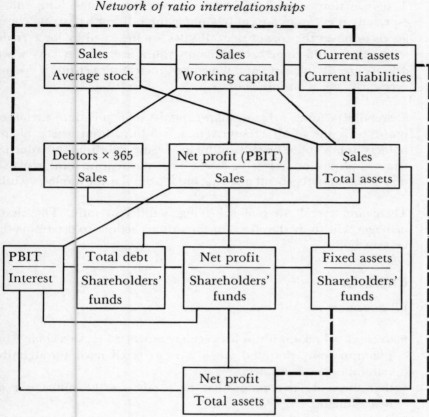

The make-up of ratios

Another way of looking at the interaction of ratios is to look behind them for their make-up. For instance, the return on capital employed ratio is made up of net profit and shareholders' funds. Net profit is found in the profit and loss account. Shareholders' funds is found on the balance sheet.

Net profit or net earnings is the result of subtracting the cost of sales, the operating expenses, the interest charges and tax from the sales. All these four costs or expenses are made up of individual items that could be reduced to increase the net profit. Also, sales could be increased.

Look to the reason why a ratio has changed. The ratio may be better, but the reason for the change may not be so good.

67

The reduction method may cause a problem in the long run – especially if expenses are cut by not paying bills, or by buying cheap goods to lower the cost of sales. If sales are increased by loose credit terms, this could come back to haunt you a few months later when debtors greatly increase. And remember, increasing net profit doesn't necessarily mean an inflow of cash.

Shareholders' funds – that is, share capital + share premium + retained profits – is the result of subtracting liabilities from assets. Shareholders' funds could be reduced by increasing liabilities, or reducing retained profits, or decreasing assets. This may require some explanation at the annual general meeting, but it's the way the numbers work.

There are several ways of achieving a different ratio. The clever manager will study the effects of the various actions to determine the best method.

Checklist

I'll remember . . .

- to check all relationships between ratios when I make a change for planning purposes, and when a ratio is changed through the natural order of business.
- that there are five ratios that have sales as the numerator or denominator.
- that a ratio may be changed three ways: change the numerator, the denominator, or both.
- that a good change in one ratio may be bad for the overall business.
- that a balance is necessary to have a healthy business.
- to check the ratio relationship diagram when I am thinking about a change.
- that most ratios are made up of many accounting transactions from the balance sheet or the profit and loss account.

◀ CHAPTER 6 ▶

FINANCIAL PLANNING

Effective decisions are crucial to job status and promotions. They require the ability to make forecasts and think ahead. Forecasts are sometimes called 'what if' exercises.

Analytical management techniques are particularly important for 'financial' planning.

Anything involving the use of company funds normally requires strong justification. If borrowing is contemplated, this means spending time with your financial people and/or a banker. You'll need to prepare detailed financial information, such as the discounted rate of return and the cost of capital. You will also need to spend time with your marketing department to perform sales research, and with the engineers to check building costs. All this takes time and money.

This part of the book presents three quick decision-shaping tools. These tools will help you to establish if you are in the ball park, whether there is a chance of an appropriate payback, and if the project is worth spending the time and effort to prepare a detailed proposal for top management.

The three planning tools are:

1. Break-even analysis (for product planning)
2. Decision-tree analysis (for building or equipment)
3. Cost-benefit analysis (for capital purchases).

Break-even analysis

Break-even analysis can give a strong indication of the probability of a project being profitable.

Break-even analysis is a good, cheap screening technique. It can help you to determine whether or not it's worthwhile to do a more intensive and costly analysis.

Break-even analysis provides a handle for designing product specifications. For example, each design has implications for cost. Costs obviously affect price and marketing feasibility. Break-even analysis lets you compare the costs and prices of various designs before the specifications are frozen. Using break-even analysis, you can first test the feasibility of a new product on paper, rather than actually going into production and testing the market.

Break-even analysis can be a substitute for estimating an unknown factor in making project decisions. If most expenses are known, the other two variables, profit and demand, may be varied. The analysis can help to determine the cash flow, the level of demand needed, and what combination of price and demand will yield the hoped-for profit.

For instance, let's suppose a manager at JOG Limited has an idea for a new product. He wants to get a quick feel of its feasibility and break-even point. The following examples will provide two means for doing this: by a formula and by a graph.

Break-even formula
The formula is:

Break-even sales = fixed costs + variable costs
$$Be = F + V$$

Example 1
Suppose the fixed costs are £100,000, and the variable costs are 66.7 per cent of the break-even sales.

$$Be = £100,000 + 66.7\%Be$$

By simple algebra,

$$Be - 66.7\%Be = £100,000$$

$$33.3\%Be = £100,000$$
$$Be = \frac{£100,000}{33.3\%}$$
$$Be = £300,000 \text{ (by rounding)}$$

Example 2

Now suppose the fixed costs have doubled to £200,000, and the variable costs are 55 per cent of the break-even sales.

$$Be = £200,000 + 55\%Be$$

By simple algebra,

$$Be - 55\%Be = £200,000$$
$$45\%Be = £200,000$$
$$Be = \frac{£200,000}{45\%}$$
$$Be = £445,000 \text{ (by rounding)}$$

Break-even graphs

Let's look again at the first example. The fixed costs are £100,000 and the variable costs are 66.7 per cent of the break-even sales. Suppose the selling price of the product is £7.50 per unit. The following graph plots (a) sales revenue and (b) production cost against the number of units produced. Where the two lines cross is the break-even point.

If the fixed costs are £200,000 and the variable costs are 55 per cent of the break-even sales, we have the following graph.

Margin of safety

Break-even analysis can also help to determine a margin of safety. To do this, subtract the break-even sales revenue from the total sales revenue and divide by the total sales revenue. For instance, suppose the sales of the new product are 275,000 units. The product sells at £7.50, so the total sales revenue is £7.50 × 275,000 = £2,062,500.

What is your room for manoeuvre? Bankers will not be convinced unless you have considered the worst possible scenario.

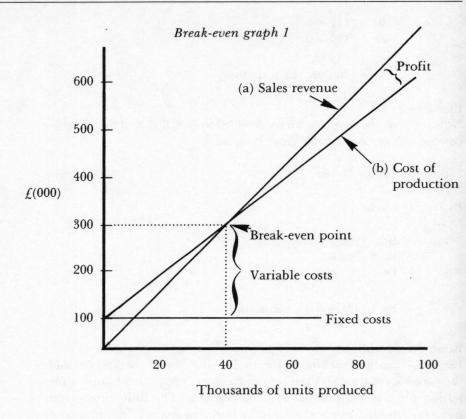

Break-even graph 1

Example 1
The fixed expenses are £100,000. As we previously calculated, the break-even sales revenue is approximately £300,000.

$$£2,062,500 - £300,000 \; = \; \frac{£1,762,500}{£2,062,500} \; = \; 85\% \text{ safety margin}$$

Example 2
The fixed expenses are £200,000, and the break-even sales revenue is approximately £445,000.

$$£2,062,500 - £445,000 \; = \; \frac{£1,617,500}{£2,062,500} \; = \; 78\% \text{ safety margin}$$

The higher fixed expenses resulted in a lower margin of safety, because

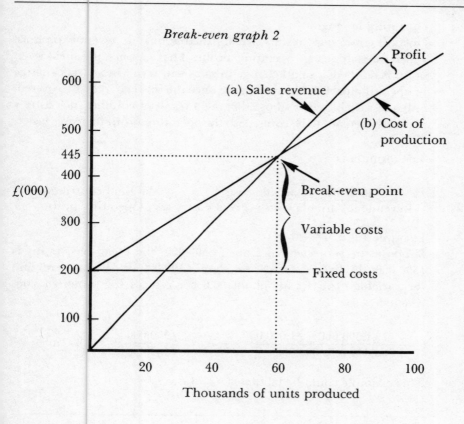

Break-even graph 2

the break-even point required more sales. This shows that the principle of leverage (discussed in the next section) works two ways. During good sales times it provides more profit; during slow sales times, the fixed expenses can be a burden.

Leverage

Break-even analysis helps with leverage calculations which relate changes in sales to changes in income. There are two types of leverage: operating and financial. Operating leverage comes from having higher fixed expenses, such as maintenance, rent and some utilities. Financial leverage results from interest payments on debt incurred by borrowing or by issuing bonds.

Projects must cover their fixed costs.

Operating leverage

Operating leverage results when fluctuations in revenue produce wider fluctuations in operating profit. That is, once the break-even point is reached, a small change in sales will result in a larger change in operating profit. This is because once the fixed charges are covered, only the variable costs (those that are a result of volume, such as raw materials) remain to be covered, so the operating profit increases faster.

The formula is:

$$\frac{\text{Revenue} - \text{Variable costs}}{\text{Revenue} - \text{Variable costs} - \text{Fixed costs}} = \frac{\text{Marginal contribution}}{\text{Operating profit}}$$

Example 1

Suppose the projected sales are £1,500,000; the break-even point is £300,000; the fixed expenses are about £100,000 or 33.3 per cent, and the variable expenses are about 66.6 per cent of the projected sales revenue.

$$\frac{£1,500,000 - £1,000,000}{£1,500,000 - £1,000,000 - £100,000} = \frac{£500,000}{£400,000} = 1.25 \text{ times}$$

This example could be tabulated as follows:

Units sold	Sales (£)	Operating expenses (£)	Operating profit (PBIT) (£)
0	0	100,000	(−100,000)
40,000	300,000	300,000	0
100,000	750,000	600,000	150,000
200,000	1,500,000	1,100,000	400,000
300,000	2,250,000	1,600,000	650,000

Example 2

The projected sales are £1,500,000; the break-even point is £445,000; the fixed expenses are about £200,000 or 45 per cent of the break-even revenue; and the variable expenses are about 55 per cent of the projected sales revenue. (Rounding to even numbers is used to keep the calculation simple.)

$$\frac{£1,500,000 - £825,000}{£1,500,000 - £825,000 - £200,000} = \frac{£675,000}{£475,000} = 1.42 \text{ times}$$

This results in about a 19 per cent increase in operating income from when fixed expenses were doubled on the same amount of sales revenue.

Units sold	Sales (£)	Operating expenses (£)	Operating profit (PBIT) (£)
0	0	200,000	(−200,000)
60,000	445,000	445,000	0
100,000	750,000	613,000	137,000
200,000	1,500,000	1,026,000	474,000
300,000	2,250,000	1,439,000	811,000

Leverage varies at each level of production because of the changing weight fixed expenses have to total expenses. Operating leverage decreases as the company's sales increase. Other things being equal, the higher a firm's operating leverage, the higher its risk.

The higher the ratio of fixed costs to variable costs, the higher the risk.

These examples may also be graphed. Break-even graph 1, in the previous section, shows a gap between the sales–revenue line and the cost-of-production line for production greater than 40,000 units.

On break-even graph 2, the gap begins after 60,000 units. Graph 2 shows more leverage than graph 1.

Remember, if sales revenue does not materialise to cover the increase in fixed expenses, JOG Limited will make losses faster than if it had a lower break-even point.

High financial leverage is a very risky strategy. Companies with such a strategy should be avoided by those seeking security.

Financial leverage
Financial leverage results from the use of funds in return for a fixed payment, such as an interest payment. The greater the degree that interest expenses are covered, the lower the degree of financial leverage.

The higher the use, the more the leverage – and the greater the risk placed on the ordinary shareholders. Financial leverage is determined by:

$$\frac{\text{Revenue} - \text{Variable cost} - \text{Fixed cost}}{\text{Revenue} - \text{Variable cost} - \text{Fixed cost} - \text{Interest}} = \frac{\text{Operating profit}}{\text{Profit before tax}}$$

JOG Limited's profit and loss account showed interest payments of £278,000. Let's use this number in connection with the two different operating leverage ratios we just worked and see if it makes a difference.

Example 1

$$\frac{£1,500,000 - £1,000,000 - £100,000}{£1,500,000 - £1,000,000 - £100,000 - £278,000} =$$

$$\frac{£400,000}{£122,000} = 3.27 \text{ times}$$

Example 2

$$\frac{£1,500,000 - £825,000 - £200,000}{£1,500,000 - £825,000 - £200,000 - £278,000} = \frac{£475,000}{£197,000} = 2.41 \text{ times}$$

In the first example the increase was from 1.25 times to 3.27 times. In the second example, the increase was from 1.42 times to 2.41 times. The difference in the increase in financial leverage from operating leverage is the greater coverage of the fixed costs in Example 1.

Now let's combine these two formulas and see what occurs when we have two types of leverage working for us – or against us, as during periods of low sales.

The combined formula is:

$$\frac{\text{Revenue} - \text{Variable cost}}{\text{Revenue} - \text{Variable cost} - \text{Fixed cost}} \times$$

$$\frac{\text{Revenue} - \text{Variable cost} - \text{Fixed cost}}{\text{Revenue} - \text{Variable cost} - \text{Fixed cost} - \text{Interest}} =$$

$$\frac{\text{Revenue} - \text{Variable cost}}{\text{Revenue} - \text{Variable cost} - \text{Fixed cost} - \text{Interest}} =$$

$$\frac{\text{Marginal contribution}}{\text{Profit before tax}}$$

Substituting the figures from the first example:

$$\frac{£1,500,000 - £1,000,000}{£1,500,000 - £1,000,000 - £100,000 - £278,000} = \frac{£500,000}{£122,000} = 4.1 \text{ times}$$

And the second example:

$$\frac{£1,500,000 - £825,000}{£1,500,000 - £825,000 - £200,000 - £278,000} = \frac{£675,000}{£197,000} = 3.4 \text{ times}$$

Drawbacks to using break-even analysis

Break-even analysis does not permit proper examination of cash flow. One appropriate way to make investment or capital-purchasing decisions is to consider the proposed project's cash flow. If the discounted value of the cash flow exceeds the required cash outlay then the project is acceptable, other things being equal.

Break-even analysis has its limitations.

The use of break-even analysis requires that many restrictive assumptions about cost-revenue relationships be made. It is basically a negative technique, defining constraints rather than looking at benefits.

Break-even analysis is static. It is good for a single point in time, not a period of time.

There are alternative uses for money in any business. This technique considers only one at a time and it does not compare them.

The break-even analysis technique is quite simplistic. It is good for getting a feel and for determining if further study is feasible. But it should not be used for final decisions.

Leverage means risk, and risk under a period of high sales is heavily rewarded. But with low sales it becomes a heavy burden to pay for fixed costs with little sales revenue.

Decision-tree analysis

Decision tree analysis helps with the logic of decision making.

Decision-tree analysis can be a useful tool for the decision maker. By combining decision points with probabilities and costs, better information is available.

It should be possible in most decisions to look at a variety of alternatives, even some with follow-on decisions.

For example, you may want to build a modular plant for later expansion, or increment your new plant construction to take advantage of later information. Or you may want to examine the pay-off of building a large plant now. This is what decision-tree analysis helps you to do. It permits each decision point to have more than one choice. If these decision points are charted, they appear as branches – hence the name 'decision tree'. (See the diagram on page 82.)

The following example illustrates some of the uses of decision-tree analysis.

Example of decision-tree analysis
You want to determine whether to build a large or small building.

Probability analysis is only as useful as the 'thought' that has gone into the assumptions behind it.

First, gather information concerning the cost of each building size. A large building would cost £6 million and a small one £4 million. The expected income from the large building is £12 million if there is a high demand, and £7 million if the demand is low. The income from the small building would be £8 million for a high demand and £7 million for a low demand.

Next, arrange the information in a matrix as shown below (m = millions).

	Large building			Small building		
	Income	*Cost*	*Return*	*Income*	*Cost*	*Return*
High demand	£12m	– £6m	= £6m	£8m	– £4m	= £4m
Low demand	£7m	– £6m	= £1m	£7m	– £4m	= £3m

Now you need to determine whether there will be a high or low demand. This may be done through your own experience, the opinions of various trade associations, your marketing group, universities, suppliers, customers, competitors, trade magazines or business magazines and newspapers.

From this information, probabilities are assigned as to whether there will be a high or low demand and how strongly you believe it. Let's assume the probability of a high demand would be 60 per cent or 0.6, and the probability of a low demand would be 40 per cent or 0.4.

The following matrix shows the expected profit (m = millions).

	High demand		Low demand		
	Probability	*Return*	*Probability*	*Return*	*Pay-off*
Large building	0.6	× £6m	+ 0.4	× £1m	= £4m
Small building	0.6	× £4m	+ 0.4	× £3m	= £3.6m

In this instance, building the large building would be more profitable than building the small building by a difference of £4m – £3.6m = £400,000. With this information a better decision can be made.

The probabilities reflect uncertainty of decision making. By using various probabilities you can usually arrive at a ball-park figure that makes sense to you.

As an exercise, let's go back and see what the difference is if the probabilities are reversed: The probability of a high demand is 0.4 and the probability of a low demand is 0.6. Calculate the pay-off for each type of building, and write the figures in the matrix below.

	High demand		Low demand		
	Probability	*Return*	*Probability*	*Return*	*Pay-off*
Large building	0.4	× £6m	+ 0.6	× £1m	=
Small building	0.4	× £4m	+ 0.6	× £3m	=

How would this affect your decision?

Decision-tree analysis is most useful for analysing complex situations where there are numerous alternatives.

Now let's consider that you may have more than one decision point. For instance, you might be able to build a small building that can be expanded at a later date if demand increases. This time there is an additional decision point for the small building. You will have three pay-offs to compare instead of two: the total pay-off for the large building, the total pay-off for the small building, and the total pay-off for a small building that can be expanded.

We have previously determined the pay-off for a large building and a small building with no expansion capabilities, based on a 60 per cent probability of high demand and a 40 per cent probability of low demand. We calculated that for a large building the pay-off is £4 million and for a small building the pay-off is £3.6 million.

Assume that the cost of expanding the small building is £3 million. High demand would give an income of £12 million, from which we subtract the £4 million initial building cost and the £3 million expansion cost, for a pay-off of £5 million. We have to multiply this figure by 60 per cent, as we believe there is only a 60 per cent chance of a high demand. This gives us a high-demand pay-off of £3 million for the expanded small building. If there is a low demand, an expansion would not be warranted. In this case, the income would be £7 million minus the £4 million building cost, for a pay-off of £3 million. This times 40 per cent gives a low-demand pay-off of £1.2 million.

To find the total pay-off from a small building with expansion capabilities, we add the high-demand pay-off to the low-demand pay-off. £3 million plus £1.2 million gives a total pay-off of £4.2 million. Compare this with the large-building pay-off of £4 million and the small-building pay-off of £3.6 million. The logical choice is to build a small building with later expansion capabilities.

Cost-benefit analysis

The term 'capital budgeting' essentially means matching the available funds with the most beneficial use of those funds. This should provide a common basis for evaluating investment opportunities and projects for the company.

Capital budgeting also means that the benefit is for the long term – more than one yar. This applies to buildings and equipment as well as research and public relations enhancement. A quick way to compare two different proposals or projects, especially if they are for tangible items, is a cost-benefit analysis. This measures the relationship between anticipated returns and costs. The cost-benefit analysis measures the anticipated return on investment. The example below compares the costs and benefits of purchasing new equipment. Assume that the new equipment will raise the production cost from 90p to £1.00 per unit.

> Costs can nearly always be quantified. Benefits sometimes are of a more qualitative nature.

	Current equipment	New equipment
Units produced annually	100,000	125,000
Sales value at £1.50 per unit	£150,000	£187,000
Direct cost of the units produced	90,000	125,000
Gross profit	£60,000	£62,500
Annual benefit		£2,500

Assuming constant sales, the total benefit is the annual benefit of £2,500 multiplied by the useful life of the new equipment. These quick calculations should be discounted by the expected inflation rate to get a discounted rate of return over the years of useful life or expected income.

Decision tree

Start from the bottom and work upwards to the pay-offs.

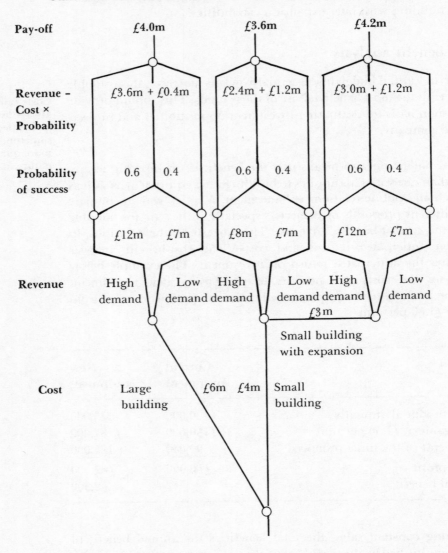

| Pay-off | £4.0m | £3.6m | £4.2m |

Revenue –
Cost ×
Probability

£3.6m + £0.4m £2.4m + £1.2m £3.0m + £1.2m

Probability
of success

0.6 0.4   0.6 0.4   0.6 0.4

Revenue

£12m £7m   £8m £7m   £12m £7m

High demand   Low demand   High demand   Low demand   High demand   Low demand

£3m

Small building
with expansion

Cost

Large building   £6m £4m   Small building

The figures can be adjusted for probability of success, taking the discounted income times the probability of success. For instance, if the new equipment has a useful life of 5 years and the income is discounted by 10 per cent, the costs and benefits of purchasing it will be as shown in the table overleaf.

If the cost of the new equipment, installation, disruption, training, etc, minus the scrap value is less than the risk, it probably should be considered for investment and more study.

Review

True or False? Write **T** or **F** in the spaces below.

— 1. Break-even analysis is an expensive and time-consuming tool.
— 2. Break-even analysis can be used for product design, equipment purchase and production analysis.
— 3. All financial planning tools have some shortcomings and should not be used for final decisions.
— 4. Decision-tree analysis helps to understand the feasibility of constructing different size buildings.
— 5. Cost-benefit analysis does not allow you to take into account the probabilities or the discounted rate of return.

Answers: 1 F, 2 T, 3 T, 4 T, 5 F.

Match each formula to its definition by connecting them with a line.

Formula		Definition
1. $\dfrac{\text{Revenue} - \text{Variable costs}}{\text{Revenue} - \text{Variable costs} - \text{Fixed costs}}$	A.	$\dfrac{\text{Operating profit}}{\text{Profit before tax}}$
2. $\dfrac{\text{Revenue} - \text{Variable costs} - \text{Fixed costs}}{\text{Revenue} - \text{Variable costs} - \text{Fixed costs} - \text{Interest}}$	B.	$\dfrac{\text{Marginal contribution}}{\text{Earnings before tax}}$
3. $\dfrac{\text{Revenue} - \text{Variable costs}}{\text{Revenue} - \text{Variable costs} - \text{Fixed costs} - \text{Interest}}$	C.	$\dfrac{\text{Marginal contribution}}{\text{Operating profit}}$

Answers: 1 C, 2 A, 3 B.

| Year | Fairly certain | | | Moderate | | | Risky | | |
	Income	Probability of success	New	Income	Probability of success	New	Income	Probability of success	New
1	£2,500	1.0	£2,500	£2,500	1.0	£2,500	£2,500	0.9	£2,250
2	2,065	1.0	2,065	2,065	0.9	1,859	2,065	0.8	1,652
3	1,878	1.0	1,878	1,878	0.8	1,502	1,878	0.7	1,315
4	1,708	1.0	1,708	1,708	0.7	1,196	1,708	0.6	1,025
5	1,553	1.0	1,553	1,553	0.6	932	1,553	0.5	777
	£9,704		£9,704	£9,704		£7,989	£9,704		£7,019

Choose A, B or C by ticking the appropriate box.

1. Break-even analysis helps to
   □ **A.** compute costs and benefits.
   □ **B.** determine probabilities.
   □ **C.** understand how many units of a product we must sell before we begin to realise a profit.

2. The two types of leverage are
   □ **A.** balance sheet and profit and loss account.
   □ **B.** high and low.
   □ **C.** operational and financial.

3. Decision-tree analysis helps you to
   □ **A.** determine pay-off for two or more alternatives under various economic conditions.
   □ **B.** determine what trees to plant at your corporation.
   □ **C.** determine the break-even point.

4. Decision-tree analysis involves the use of
   □ **A.** cost and revenue.
   □ **B.** cost, revenue and demand.
   □ **C.** cost, revenue and probable demand.

5. Cost-benefit analysis measures
   □ **A.** the cost of a project.
   □ **B.** the anticipated returns and costs.
   □ **C.** the returns of any project.

6. Cost-benefit analysis
   □ **A.** can make use of probabilities.
   □ **B.** can be used to measure your popularity.
   □ **C.** is the discounted rate of return

Answers: 1 C, 2 C, 3 A, 4 C, 5 B, 6 A.

CHAPTER 7

HOW TO READ AN ANNUAL REPORT

The annual report to the shareholders generally looks to the past, and it is in management's best interest to present the company in a good light. Therefore expect to read a lot of positive words. Also, some auditors seem not to be as independent as they pretend. Their reports tend to offer only vague assurances that the annual accounts are correctly stated. They use the phrase 'a true and fair view' which does not mean that the accounts are absolutely accurate, only that they are roughly in the right ball park. They do not comment on every accountancy policy or the provisions in the accounts. Since different policies can produce very different figures this omission by the audit report is unhelpful for interpreting the accounts of any company. Indeed, the number of recent well-publicised failures of large companies in the UK, all of which had been receiving unqualified audit reports on their accounts in the years prior to their collapse, points up this failing by the audit profession.

However, annual reports do have their place, and if properly used they can supply a lot of inside information. Annual reports are valuable to:

- Managers within the company
- Creditors
- Potential and current investors
- Potential and current customers and suppliers.

Company managers usually have their own detailed statements. Their particular area may be only one line on a consolidated statement in the annual report, but their area figures are a part of the consolidated statement.

Potential investors, creditors and suppliers will certainly want to know the debt situation and how fast the company pays its bills and collects its debts. They should also keep up with stories and articles concerning their industry and any analysis a stockbroker may supply.

An annual report is usually divided into the following sections:

- The chairman's statement
- The directors report
- The auditor's report
- Balance sheet, profit and loss account and the source and application of funds statement
- The notes to the accounts.

Begin with the audit report

The report by the auditors is usually at the front of the financial accounts, directly before the balance sheet. This is the best place to start as it is an independent report by the auditors to the shareholders which passes judgement, or offers an opinion, as to the reliability of the figures included in the financial statements. If there is anything more than the usual two paragraph standard statement using phrases such as 'in accordance with auditing standards' or 'the financial statements give a true and fair view' and 'properly prepared in accordance with the Companies Act . . .' then you should pay very close attention to the qualifications the auditors give.

It is unusual to find qualifications in the accounts of the big blue-chip companies, or, for that matter, in the accounts of well-regulated smaller companies. A qualification really can be a health warning to outsiders. The only exception to this general rule is insurance companies who, for largely academic reasons, can rarely get a completely clean audit report.

In theory the shareholder is the auditor's client. In practice it tends to be company directors' wishes that auditors respond to.

On the other hand, a clean audit report is a good sign that things are probably well with the company.

Accounting policies

Next, go to the accounting policies and look to see if the company has changed accounting principles or methods. When a company changes its accounting method, it may be trying to make the figures look better. For instance, has the depreciation period been extended? Is it because the assets haven't been working as hard as they first thought and now they will have a longer life? It could be that sales haven't grown as projected. Sometimes the whole story is told in the notes to the accounts. There must be sufficient notes to explain clearly, but not enough to obfuscate.

Analyse accounting policies carefully. Check them for inconsistency with the previous year's report.

Another reason to change accounting methods is that earnings are up because of a windfall that won't happen again and management wants to store part of it for when sales are down or to stretch out tax payments. Or are earnings down because of a change in accounting, not sales? This, by the way, may be good.

A set of accounts is supposed to be prepared using consistent policies between one year and the next. However, in practice this is often not the case. Sometimes accounting policies will be changed for reasons of expediency. The directors have noticed that they can take more profit earlier (say this year as compared with next year, or the year after) and may decide to do so, not because this reflects more fairly the true position of the company, but because it suits their own purposes and careers.

Less cynically, the new policy may be fairer, or it may have hitherto unrealised tax advantages.

In any case a change in accounting policy will require careful consideration of the impact the change will have upon the performance of the company when compared with previous years, and when comparing the company with other companies in the same industry.

Below are shown a number of items regularly included in the accounts of companies, and appearing in the notes, together with some explanation of what they may really mean.

Revaluations. This particularly applies to property, both freehold and long-term leasehold. These will have resulted in paper profits only, unless they have been, or are likely to be sold off. Directors whose companies have freehold properties tend to fall over themselves to have the properties revalued in times of rising property values. They may be very quiet about the subject in times of falling values.

Deferred income. This is quite a fair method of accounting for income and the associated profit in the period in which the work is done instead of the period in which the contract for the work may have been signed (and indeed the payment received from the customer). Examples will include the construction industry or the publishing industry where down payments or royalties are paid in advance. It can be misused to make this year look less profitable so that next year will look that much better. New management taking over at the end of one financial year would be interested in such a scheme to make the previous management look worse, and by comparison, themselves look better in the following year.

Extraordinary items. Items giving rise to profit from unusual sources such as the sale of assets (eg property) should be shown separately, because they are not part of the normal business and would distort trends analysis if left unexplained.

Depreciation. There are various methods of depreciation as shown in an earlier chapter. An asset-intensive business, where depreciation forms a significant proportion of the total expenses, can significantly alter its profit by changing from one perfectly legitimate policy for depreciation to another.

Provisions. Provisions can be made against a wide variety of balances. Most, if not all, provisions are subjective in nature. There is always room to debate the scope of a provision if not the need to make a provision in the first place. Pending litigation is always an area where provisions against profit can be made. As in the earlier example this profit can be clawed back next year after the case has finished.

Provision against doubtful debts is another example where there is an opportunity to change the figures and disguise the real situation.

Financial statements

Interpreting financial statements is about making comparisons between this year and last year, and other similar companies.

Next move to the balance sheet and profit and loss account and compare the ratios of all the years presented. Pay particular attention to debtors and stock. If the report doesn't furnish the ratios, you ought to do them yourself. Ask questions, like: Are debtors and stocks growing faster than sales? Does this mean the company is trying to increase or maintain sales through a lax credit policy? Is the company keeping the plant operating at a higher level without sales, or is this a stocking up prior to the big sales season? Check the current ratio and see if the company is paying on time and has an aggressive debtors collection policy.

Another area to watch is long-term debt. It may be expanding; if the company is growing this is usually good. However, if sales are levelling out it may not be so good.

Also, check asset values by comparing them with those of similar companies. Are they overestimated? Is there an explanation? Remember that overestimated asset values, even with logical reasons, are really not too meaningful without eager buyers.

Look for differences. This means comparing one year with another and the current annual report with past reports. Look for cash flow over time and what is done with it. Is the money reinvested, paid out in dividends, or paying off heavy debt? Remember, a lot depends on the industry, the age of the company, and the business cycle.

Check the turnover figure. Are sales increasing, remaining steady, or dropping off? If the sales figures are dropping off, this may signal trouble. Sales should keep up with inflation. But they may be down for legitimate reasons – for example, if part of the company was sold. That part may have been unprofitable, and even with lower sales, profits may be up.

Some people go immediately to earnings per share (EPS). But this figure can be misleading if part of the corporation has been sold, or if there has been a decrease in advertising or research and development, or if there has been a postponement of some expenses that cause the earnings to rise. Also, earnings per share will vary under different accounting methods. They do not reflect risk to the company or a division of the company. Earnings per share do not account for the investment required for working capital or fixed capital needs. So if these needs or expenses are curtailed to make the earnings look good in the short term, be careful about the long term.

Chairman's statement

The next place to look is the chairman's statement. This will provide clues about the workings of the company. It should be in tune with what you have already found out. In the statement, watch for weak words, such as 'we're working on it', 'continuing towards', 'nearly complete', 'considered to be', and 'except for'. Also watch for words that sound like an apology, or that are more modifiers than action words when the writer analyses changes in sales debt, or profit.

The chairman's statement will usually only mention the good views. You will have to look elsewhere to get a balanced view.

The statement should explain in easily understood language what has happened, where the company is going, how it will get there, and why. A lot don't. A good one will tell it like it is, including any difficulties. This type of statement may run to many pages – but really good statements are rare.

Explanations and analysis

Finally, look at the explanations and analysis provided. Note whether new share capital has been issued and what the proceeds were used for. Was it used to expand the plant to meet improving sales? Or was it used to pay off debt? If possible, see how much stock is held by the company officers and board members. Are they buying or selling? Also check for the qualifications of top management, if available.

Look for legal disputes. Have they been settled? Who are they with – the Inland Revenue, creditors or customers? Note how long they have been going on. Almost any company may have a sound reason to disagree with a government department, but a dispute with a creditor or a customer may signal trouble.

In general, auditors do their jobs right. They do not provide approval or endorsements for the company. They only provide reasonable assurance that the numbers presented do not intentionally distort the company's financial position.

Checklist

- I will check the annual report by starting with the auditors' report.
- I will watch for weak words such as 'subject to', 'working on it', 'nearly complete' and 'except for'.
- I will compare the past 5–10 years' ratios to obtain a better understanding of what has really happened.
- I will keep up with business press reports, especially those affecting my industry.
- I will be careful if there are numerous footnotes.

◀ FURTHER READING
FROM KOGAN PAGE ▶

Accounting for Non-Accountants, Graham Mott
Baffled by Balance Sheets? William Lee Johnson
Budgeting, Terry Dickey
The Cash Collection Action Kit, Philip Gegan and Jane Harrison
How to Understand Financial Statements, James O Gill
How to Understand the Financial Press, John Andrew

A full list is available from the publishers; telephone 071-278 0433 or
fax 071-837 6348.